X-ray Way to Master Golf

Ken Adwick

X-ray Way
to
Master Golf

KEN ADWICK

As told to James Green
With photographs By Frank Sowerby

PELHAM BOOKS

First published in Great Britain by
Pelham Books Ltd.
52 Bedford Square
London, W.C.1
1970

7207 0367 0

Set and printed in Great Britain by
Hollen Street Press Ltd., Slough, Bucks,
in eleven on thirteen point Baskerville,
and bound by James Burn at Esher, Surrey

To
my wife Joan

FOREWORD
by NEIL COLES

(A Ryder Cup player, Dunlop Master and winner of many tournaments, he has for years been one of the leading money winners in British golf.)

I have more reason than most to appreciate Ken Adwick's worth as a golfer and as a teaching professional since I started with him as an assistant when I was 18-years-old.

Frankly, my golf wasn't very good when I joined him and he was able to put my golf and swing on the right path. I am pleased to have the opportunity to acknowledge that fact here.

Ken is well-known to his fellow professionals and I have no hesitation in saying that he is among the best half-a-dozen golf teachers in Britain. He's also been an extremely good player himself.

He has studied the game in depth and I can recommend that whatever golfing advice he gives is worth thinking about and acting on.

His X-ray development has created a lot of interest among amateur and professionals alike. Bernard Hunt, for instance, has told me on two or three occasions that his own X-ray pictures had taught him a lot and proved a great help.

George Will is another tournament competitor who has remarked to me about the value of the X-ray technique. He said he had guessed about certain aspects of his swing and the pictures had proved his thinking to be right.

There is no doubt that these X-rays are a step forward in widening our knowledge of the game.

As a Master golfer myself I wish Ken Adwick good luck with his book. It is teachers like Ken we are going to need to produce the new generation of Master golfers.

Contents

Illustrations

My thanks to *Golf World* for permission to draw on some of the articles I have written for that magazine and also to golfer and artist George Stokes for the various excellent illustrations he has provided.

KEN ADWICK

INTRODUCING THE AUTHOR

Ken Adwick has spent his entire life—apart from wartime service as an RAF navigator and bomb aimer—on a golf course.

He only just escaped from being born on one.

To be precise, he arrived in a house backing on to the 17th green at Birmingham's Copt Heath course where his father, W. H. "Bill" Adwick, was then the professional.

Really he had little chance to avoid becoming a full-time golfer. The game is in the Adwick family blood, and so far five members of the family have turned professional.

It all started with Uncle Jim Adwick who was one of the first members of the Professional Golfers' Association back in 1901. Then came his brother, Ken's Dad.

Cousin Tom Hassell became No 3, and Ken himself was No 4. Now Ken's eldest son, Stewart, has taken up a full-time professional appointment in Sweden.

And before closing the list I should warn that Ken's youngest son, Kelvin, although still a pink-cheeked schoolboy, is making threatening noises about the game.

Already he's won three youth cups and when he partners Ken in father and son competitions is not above offering advice about the next shot to be played!

Ken Adwick is a man's man. A broad-shouldered genial giant who looks much how one imagines a professional sportsman ought to look.

He stands six-foot-three in a pair of size twelves, weighs 17-stone, and when he wraps his Carnera-size hands around the shaft of a golf club you get some idea of how puny a cricket bat must have seemed to the late and lamented W. G. Grace.

The Adwicks are a Yorkshire family and the name originates from a village there.

Uncle Jim, now dead, started off the golf chain reaction when he became a caddy at Lindrick. For his first club he actually cut a stick out of a hedge for the shaft.

Around the turn of the Century he was a first-class player and for nearly 40 years was professional at the Olton club.

He knew all the old-time greats and would entertain young Ken with stories about his matches against, to drop a few names, James Braid, J. H. Taylor, Harry Vardon, Ted Ray, Abe Mitchell and Archie Compston.

As a lad Ken remembers Uncle Jim warning him not to fall for the then fashionable theory to have the club face shut at the top of the backswing.

Bill Adwick, Ken's father, was a pro at 18 at Trentham Park, Staffordshire—almost certainly the youngest professional in Britain at that time.

He was a good player but might have been better still had he not been severely wounded during the 1914-18 war. As a result of injuries to his back and right arm he had to have a total of 17 operations. Most of his career was passed at Harborne and Marston Green in the Midlands.

Ken was Bill's only son and Dad lost no time in making him a midget set of clubs. When he was just four Ken's photograph, swinging away, was on the front pages of the national Press.

Something of an embarrassment really because he's learned a little more about golf since then and as a purist would prefer not to notice that in the picture he is holding the club with left hand under right. It is automatic with all children—try the experiment on Junior if you like. But an Adwick holding the club like that!

"From that moment I was the black sheep of the family," he regrets.

By six or seven he was playing more orthodoxly and at fifteen was off two handicap and competing in the English Boys' Championship.

They understood his ability and ambitions well enough at his school. It must have helped that Ken was already playing one of his teachers and beating him.

As a result he was officially allowed to play golf instead of other sports—although he did mix in some rugby during the winter. But as they knew golf would be his love and living they decided not to fight it.

By 1939 he was scratch and an assistant professional at Sutton Coldfield earning all of 7s 6d a week, less stamp money. The war took him away and when he returned to the game in 1945 it was as a full-time pro.

Due to the lost war years his golf never came easily and he had to work for his results. He used to practise for two hours a day and at night turned the garage into a practice net by stringing up an old blanket.

This dedication paid off immediately, because he went out to win the

Midland championship of 1947. He has also won the Midland Challenge Bowl and Midland Foursomes, and on one occasion the name of K. W. C. Adwick led the field in the first round of the British Open. But his interest in the tournament circuit was limited as he found greater enjoyment in being a club professional and coaching.

He's played in America, Canada, Germany, Italy, France, Holland, Switzerland, Spain and Portugal, as well as throughout the British Isles.

While still competing in tournaments he admits in private that he has had his hour of glory and now treats competitions less seriously.

But with so much experience he feels he has the authority to pass on to others what he has learned about the game. In other words, he wants to give something back. He was interested enough recently to visit America and Canada to see how Old World and New World coaching methods compared but found there was little to learn.

Ken was always considered a long-hitter and in a long-driving contest clocked up one drive of 314 yards. On average, though, he reckoned to be 260–270 yards off the tee in tournaments.

He liked to watch Henry Cotton a lot and has the warmest regard for Jimmy Adams, five times Ryder Cup player, whom he considers, along with his father, his mentor.

Dad's basic advice to Ken was "Make sure you stand still while swinging."

On the subject of advice Ken says the finest he had heard came from Jimmy Adams, who was quoting the legendary Ernest Jones: "You don't make movement to move the clubhead, you move the clubhead to make movement." It's a point he will cover in his book.

For years Adwick was professional at Trentham, Letchworth and Burhill golf clubs, before taking his present post with Shooters Hill golf club on the London-Kent borders where he has settled down most happily and is ever-busy teaching.

Neil Coles, whom Ken considers the most consistent British tournament professional, was his assistant for nine years, and another tournament man, Brian Bamford, has also been his assistant.

Ken has played with or against men like Gary Player, Dai Rees, Bobby Locke, Norman Von Nida, Peter Thomson, Christie O'Connor, and many more, and for ten years was a Southern section committeeman of the P.G.A.

So his credentials can be taken for granted.

When it came to instructing his own son, Stewart, he made him spend three months, with feet together and touching, hitting golf balls using left hand only on the club. Stewart started playing as a five-year-old and later served his apprenticeship as an assistant at Burhill, St. George's Hill, and Wentworth.

As a professional in Sweden, because of climatic conditions, he has seven months golf outside, and the remainder of the year teaching inside at a golf school.

Should you get the impression that the Adwicks know something about the game, you could be right.

Since Ken has made teaching his main interest he has earned a reputation, boosted by his articles in *Golf World* and the Press, as an outstanding theorist and coach. His enthusiasm on behalf of the ever hopeful, grievously ambitious amateur is unrelenting.

Perhaps the motto in his pro shop at Shooters Hill sums up what he feels: "There's no business like golf business."

James Green.

CHAPTER ONE

Play The Game

This is a book setting out how to play the Royal and Ancient game of golf and explaining my personal theories. The first question has to be—what is golf?

Well, it's been called many things. Not all of them printable. The definition I like as much as any is that it's a game involving a lot of walking and a little bad arithmetic.

At its simplest, and golf is rarely simple although it is my hope in the following pages to strip it of so many unnecessary complications and mystiques, all we are really doing is knocking one ball measuring around one-and-a-half inches off the top of another ball measuring some 25,000 miles.

But there is more to it than that, otherwise it wouldn't be spreading so rapidly around the world with millions more hooked—or should it be sliced?—as its popularity grows.

The reason golf is booming in my view is because it's the greatest game of them all. You don't have to take my word for it. Ask any who are already playing and they will back up that statement.

And if you are thinking of taking up the game then I am confident that in no time you will become addicted, too, and appreciate just how rewarding it is.

No, let me correct that. Golf *can* be rewarding. But at other times, as any player from "tiger" to "rabbit" knows to his sorrow, it can be the most frustrating, humiliating, aggravating, cussed, mortifying, and downright bloody-minded game on earth.

Just when you think you have it licked that's when it cuts you down to size and kicks you in the teeth. But one good shot sailing right down the middle of the fairway brings the sun out again and all is forgiven.

The purpose of my book is to ensure that your game is more sunshine than cloud, more delight than despondency, and more fairway than rough.

What is also worth remembering is that apart from the playing side of golf there are innumerable benefits to be derived from the social contacts. Wherever you find a golf course in the world then you can be sure of finding friendship and companionship. I've done a full measure of globe trotting and the game definitely opens many doors.

What golf has going for it is that, unlike such sports as football, tennis, boxing, in fact the majority of sports, it is a game which through a handicapping system allows a poor player to take on a much better opponent and yet have a reasonable chance of winning.

It's a humbling and tantalizing game and whether you are managing director or junior clerk when you're on the course then you're only as good as your standard of play. It doesn't matter how much or how little money you've got, a golf swing cannot be bought. And neither can success.

It's a game that can be played from youth to old age and only recently I had yet another newcomer I was instructing tell me that he regretted every year he had lost before taking it up. How many times I have heard that!

What also appeals is that golf provides a measure of not-too-strenuous exercise over a long time rather than concentrated exercise in a short time.

Once you know the feel of a club shaft in your hands then it becomes something more than a game. It's almost a religion . . . a love-hate relationship.

It will break your heart and fill you with despair. Yet equally it will give you some of the greatest moments of your life and send you back to the daily toil feeling ten feet tall.

When you first consider golf you would think it to be an easy game. After all, you reason, all we're doing is hitting a stationary ball and taking as long as we like in setting up for the shot.

Whereas in other ball games reaction has to be instantaneous with no time for second or third thoughts. Surely it must be harder to get to and return a fast-moving tennis ball than it is to knock a golf ball straight towards the green?

Think again because, unfortunately, it just isn't so. I rate golf the most difficult game on both physical and mental levels.

There is no such thing as a good natural player. The natural golfer is the golfing rabbit.

I know, if it's any consolation, that I had to sweat away to achieve my own golfing ability. I studied theory for years, and only wish the knowledge and understanding I now have had been mine as a younger man tackling the tournament circuit!

There is a lot of nonsense written about golf and while not pretending that it is easy to play well, the game is much less difficult than some experts would have you believe.

It's worth keeping in mind that golf, certainly at club level, is played for relaxation and enjoyment. It isn't the end of the world when you pull a bad shot out of the bag.

I can imagine you thinking that there are scores of instruction books on the market already so why should mine improve on them or be any different?

That's a fair question. I know the pictures this book contains to be revolutionary and while proving many theories as fact, they also disprove some others that have been long held.

In the chapters ahead I intend to explain, among other things:

*My X-ray method of tracing the golf swing from start-to-finish in one continuous movement, and how the photographic results can be read and analysed;

*Why there is no such thing as a late hit in a good player and why late-hitting advice is so dangerous;

*The importance of hands in the game, for a player is only as good as his hands;

*How to stand up under competition pressure and why a mechanical swing, one with the pieces put together jigsaw fashion, is inferior to an even-paced repeating free swing;

*Whereas the instruction books tell you that the ball should be struck on a line from inside-to-out, I have proof to present that our top tournament professionals actually swing from slightly outside-to-in. Not that I'm asking you to copy, but more of that later;

*And while most instructors will ask you to concentrate on such varied things as head down and look at the ball, knee movement, hip swivel, elbow into your side at the end of the backswing, my personal method learned from practical experience is to ask you to think about one thing only—that being the path you wish the clubhead to take. The swing will respond to that thought. You will find that I do not comment on the positions that players are reaching in the pictures. I am more concerned with helping you to understand how they have got into those positions and explaining the force which created those movements.

My purpose is to provide a comprehensive guide to the game. I want to help the beginner get off to a good start, to introduce the club handicap golfer to a method which will cut some shots off his present handicap—goodness knows how many keen players seem to get stuck at between 12 and 18 handicap—and I also want to pass on some theory and advanced knowledge to the low-handicap man and potential champion.

If you like, my short cut to good or master golf.

Not that I'm claiming to know it all. Nobody, least of all your Hogans, Palmers and Nicklaus', will make that foolish boast. In golf one never stops learning.

But there's a lot of difference between merely hacking away optimistically and playing proper golf shots. I've got a story to illustrate that.

A stranger was asked to make up a four on the course and gave his handicap as 24, saying "I've only been playing for three months."

He went round the course like the local professional until one of his opponents protested "Are you seriously telling us that you'd never held a club in your hands until three months ago?"

To which the stranger replied: "Good God, I never said that. I started as a boy and have been playing *at it* for twenty years. But I've only been *playing* for three months!"

Before getting down to general instruction I want to explain why I was so keen to X-ray the golf swing and the method I have devised to make it possible.

After a quarter-of-a-century of giving lessons to every standard of player, I will readily admit that even to the trained eye it is almost impossible for a professional instructor (I try to avoid the word "teacher" since I don't think you can teach golf) to pick out for certain some tiny fault in a swing which is moving like lightning.

Of course the experienced pro has a good notion of what is going wrong but there remains an area of guesswork. Which requires trial-and-error over a period in order to pinpoint the fault exactly.

Even then there may still remain an element of doubt in the player's mind.

Whereas if you have a permanent tracing of the swing you can see precisely where the player has gone wrong and, most important, show him the evidence.

This removes all doubt and permits a far more rapid rate of improvement than possible under the old hit-and-miss, hit-and-slice, or hit-and-hope methods.

As so often happens the solution to the how-to-X-ray? teaser came by pure chance. I was giving a lesson to a keen mid-handicap golfer named Frank Sowerby, not knowing that he was a professional photographer.

"If I could only show you a photograph of your complete swing," I told him, "you could see for yourself what you're doing."

He thought I was joking. But giving my remark a second thought told me: "Look, I'm a photographer, surely between us we can find some way to X-ray the swing?"

That started us talking. We forgot the lesson and began exchanging ideas about how it might be possible.

As I wanted to see not only the path of the clubhead but the path of the hands as well it meant that two lights would be necessary. One on the clubhead and the other fixed to the right thumb.

We experimented for a while until I was able to secure lights to the heads of a range of clubs from driver to putter. The thumb light was a minor problem.

But at first the equipment was a little crude. At one stage we even had a third light fixed to a cap peak to tell whether the head was moving.

Eventually we dropped the head light because it caused too much of a blur—due to the head moving back as the ball was struck and forwards towards the end of the follow-through.

I have always enjoyed writing about golf but knew that my theories were controversial. I wanted those X-ray tracings in order to prove my controversial theories to be fact.

Actually results turned out far better than even I had anticipated. We not only have the complete swing in X-ray but can at the same time freeze the action at any required point without affecting the tracing.

You never got that kind of photograph in the past.

Since the early results were so informative Sowerby and I decided better equipment was needed. I made up a set of clubs with batteries in the shafts, and a battery for the hand light was strapped to the forearm. This meant that all wires were hidden.

Next we had to be sure that there was no possibility of optical illusion. We devised a method for ensuring that the player was square to the camera. The final stage was to take out a patent on the equipment.

The first X-rays Frank Sowerby took were of myself in action. These are two of them (PLATES 1 and 2) *see page 24 and 25*. One gives a front view and the other is taken from behind and looking up the line of flight.

The inside lines show the path taken by the hands, while the wider outside lines are the path of the clubhead.

My first surprise was to find that the golf swing is more egg-shaped than I had imagined—and this proved to hold true when we X-rayed various other players soon after.

I was pleased on studying my own action to note that I was swinging low on the backswing and that the clubhead stayed low through the ball

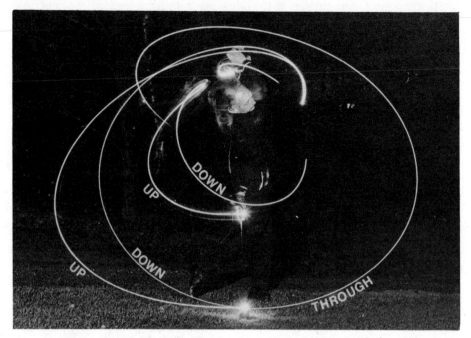

PLATE I   This is the first X-ray picture I had taken and shows my
swing path from the front view.

for a long while.

Doing that means there is less likelihood of error as you come into the
ball, while staying-with-it gives extra distance and accuracy.

I wasn't the only one excited by the breakthrough. This is what *Golf
World* wrote about the illuminated golf swing:

"It heralds the introduction of a new phase of golf instruction—a method
of allowing pupils to see exactly the path of the clubhead and hands throughout the swing in a way that has never been used before.

"Until this method was perfected the best way of seeing your own swing
was to have it filmed and then play it back in slow motion—yet even in
slow motion it is difficult to take everything in at once and within seconds
the film is finished.

"But by taking pictures in the dark with lights fixed to the clubhead
and the hands, the entire swing can be shown in one clear picture. The path
and the plane of the swing are there to be studied at leisure and a pupil can
prove to himself the difference a change of grip or stance can make to the
overall swing.

"The biggest battle in golf instruction is that the pupil can only feel what he is doing, and cannot see the results. A golfer who has always swung the club in an upright plane will feel as if he is swinging it round his knees if he flattens his swing arc by even six inches. He will feel as if his swing is very flat, but in fact it will still be quite upright.

"Yet with this latest idea in golf tuition he will be able to actually see his swing path, before and after the change. And by getting a clear picture in his mind of what he was doing and what he is trying to do the golfer is more than half-way to improving his game."

That's enough for the moment about swing analysis, except to mention that I had some amusing moments while working in my shop on the equipment.

Members would come along while I was fixing a light bulb to the top of a wooden clubhead and curiosity would get the better of them. Sooner or later they had to ask what I was doing.

Straight-faced I would reply that I had a match starting late and needed the light in order to get round once darkness fell.

Some took me seriously and said it was a wonderful idea for addressing the ball in the dark, while others made no comment but walked away shaking their head and no doubt thinking "Poor old Ken, golf has really

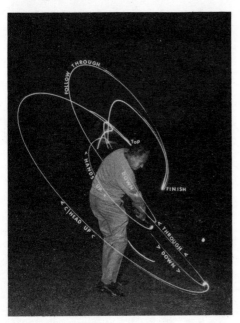

PLATE 2 Here I am swinging again. This time seen from behind and looking along the line of flight. Notice the downswing is outside the path of the upswing.

got him" and wondering when I would be permitted visitors in the local mental home.

The funniest thing happened during the days I was working on the cap peak bulb. This was lit by a battery worn on top of the head and under the cap.

One of my former pupils watched me placing the battery under my cap and scarcely daring to ask a seemingly stupid question, inquired: "That must be a device for keeping the head down. Do you sell them in the shop?"

Time for our first lesson? Let's get over to the practice ground and make a start.

CHAPTER TWO

Learning the Lesson

Even before the beginner has hit a ball I can give him some sound advice. Don't go out on the course learning to play by what are literally hit-and-miss methods.

Instead be patient and spend a little time and money with your local professional.

Believe me, after instructing hundreds of newcomers to the game, it is much easier for any coach to help a player along the right lines who knows nothing, than it is to try to put right the man who has-taught himself and on the way picked up bad golfing habits.

Correcting such a player takes twice as long. The ingrained bad habits have first to be broken down before they can be replaced with the proven basics.

It is cheaper in the long run to take lessons at the start and be guided by an expert in the playing essentials.

Equally your professional is the best man to advise you after four to six lessons about the type of clubs which will best suit your individual game.

Various things come into this, such as shaft flexibility and length, weight, and kind of club. Don't handicap yourself by purchasing an old second-hand set of clubs before taking a lesson.

For your lesson I am sure the professional will be happy to lend you a club which he thinks will suit you.

When a beginner comes to ask about golf instruction the way I start is to show him a matched set of clubs and generalise about their individual uses. (PLATE 2A) *see page 28 and 29.*

I tell him briefly that the longest club has the least loft, which makes the ball fly lower and travel farther. So the longest clubs are the ones used for gaining distance.

I then go through the set explaining the individual use of each club,

WOODS

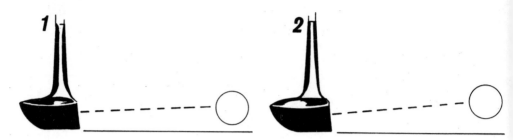

IRONS

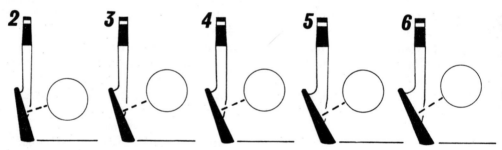

PLATE 2A   This is a typical set of clubs showing the changing lofts.

beginning with the woods.

The No 1 wood, or driver, is the lightest club of all and yet the most powerful. For many players, especially beginners, it is the most difficult to use, and for that reason it is the last club I advise any novice to pull out. Top players reckon to get around 280 to 310 yards with it according to conditions.

No 2 wood, or brassie, is the club for long fairway shots although many handicap players prefer to use it off the tee for driving. Some star professionals feel the same, while others start their round taking this club off the tee at the opening holes. Not a lot of distance is lost unless you are driving

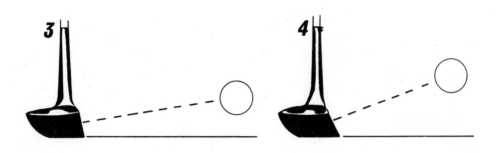

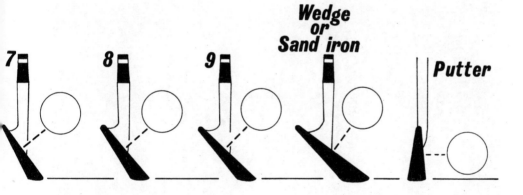

into a strong wind.

Both the No 3 wood (the spoon) and the No 4 wood can be used off the tee but are really designed for the fairway or light rough. They have more loft and get the ball up quicker—at the same time adding confidence.

No 1 and 2 irons are for the experts and most sets these days acknowledge that fact by starting off with the No 3 iron. The 1 and 2 irons really have no place in the beginners' or handicap players' bag.

No 3 and 4 irons are for distance and give greater accuracy than the woods through easier control. But some players lose confidence in their long irons and prefer to use a 5-wood.

No 5, 6 and 7 irons are the mid-irons and much favoured by the majority of golfers. They are used when the green is within range and accuracy is expected.

No 8 and 9 irons are short-distance clubs which must never be forced. Most people take to these with confidence.

The wedge is for short delicate shots over bunkers etc when pin-splitting is the object. It's a useful club also for getting out of deep rough.

The sand iron is the bunker club, and while it is possible to manufacture shots with it, it is essentially for getting out of sand traps.

Finally, the putter. Its use goes without saying.

Those then are the clubs—and so to the basis of theory, meaning the grip, stance, backswing, downswing and throughswing.

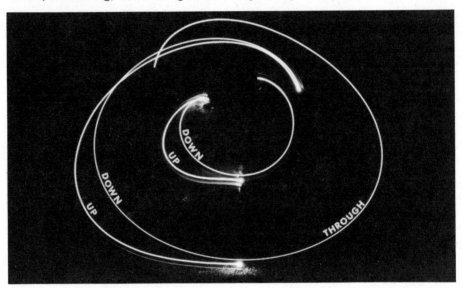

PLATE 3   This is the 20 handicap player's swing path when using his original bad grip.

The grip is vitally important because the hands are the only link between the player and the club. How the club is gripped will be reflected in the swing.

I can provide an example of that by using X-ray pictures which show what happens to the swing when the grip is altered.

PLATE 3 is of a 20-handicap man who came to me because he was not only hooking but couldn't get the ball up in the air.

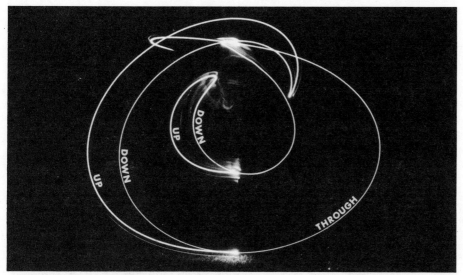

PLATE 4   The same player with his corrected grip. The back and down
swings are wider apart and the whole swing is greatly improved.

I changed him to an orthodox grip and the next picture (PLATE 4) spot-
lights the difference. His swing follows his new grip.

If you grip a club tightly it feels heavy, grip gently and it feels light.
Obviously the weight of the club doesn't change and the apparent heaviness
is due to small muscular fatigue through gripping too tightly. A too-tight
grip will produce abnormal movements to such an extent there may even
be uncontrolled trembling.

When it comes to pressure and "feel" the most important part of the
grip is the first finger and thumb of both hands. These are the most sensitive
parts of the hands—try winding a watch without using your thumb.

Finger tension is a vital part of the golf swing. Grip firm, but never vicelike. As the swing approaches the actual strike the grip becomes very firm
due to centrifugal force. It's a natural reaction.

There are three kinds of grip—starting with the Sledgehammer, which
is both hands round the shaft without overlapping. Some players with short
fingers prefer to use it.

The second is the Interlocking grip with the little finger of the right hand
coupling with the first finger of the left. This seems to be dying out as it
makes the grip too fierce.

Leaving the grip I use and recommend like most other professionals.
This is the Vardon grip, which 95 per cent of players adopt.

PLATE 6 (*opposite*) Here are five pictures on the subject of grip. 6A shows how to take up your grip with both palms opposing. 6B shows the same position once the hands have closed. This is a copybook grip. Picture 6C is a sledgehammer grip— a favourite sometimes where the player has small hands. 6D is the interlocking grip, hardly used because it is too fierce.

PLATE 5   This is the correct grip as seen by the onlooker, with the imaginary line through both "V's" pointing at right shoulder. Turn the book upside down and that is how you should see your own hands. The "V's" now appear to be pointing up the shaft.

The two inverted "V's" made by the first finger and thumb of both hands appear to the onlooker to be pointing to the right shoulder.

However, to the bird's-eye view of the player the "V's" seem to run up the middle of the shaft. This illustration (PLATE 5) shows the two different views. Simply turn the page upside down and that is how you should see your own grip.

For the Vardon grip place the left hand on the club first with the inverted "V" seeming to point up the shaft at you. Then place the right hand below the left—at the same time placing the little finger of the right hand over the first finger of the left.

The reason this is done is to give a better feel, and to take some of the power out of the right hand, which is always trying to dominate.

The first three fingers of the left hand and the "trigger" finger and thumb of the right hand are the main agents giving the feel of the club—the most sensitive spots (PLATE 6). Study these pictures because a correct grip is essential to good golf.

You may have heard a lot of talk about players showing one, two, three or four knuckles in their left hand grip.

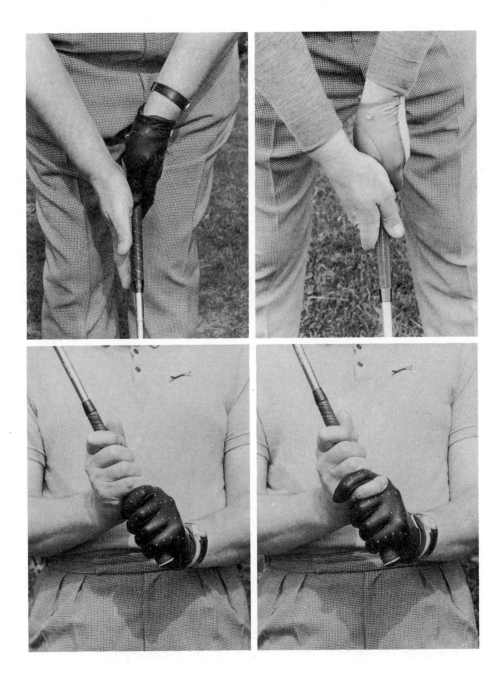

6E is the most commonly used of all —the Vardon grip. The second and fifth pictures (*see page 33*) are two different views of the same grip.

If you are showing one knuckle when looking down the shaft then it is a weak grip and wrong. The inverted "V" will point to the left shoulder.

Go to the other extreme and show four knuckles and the grip will be too strong and the "V" will point to way outside the right shoulder (PLATE 7).

But when the club is being held correctly you should be showing about two-and-a-half knuckles.

Without exception the players coming to me for advice usually have no problem over their left hand grip. But the biggest fault, *and I would say it is as high as 75 per cent of all amateur players*, is in having the right hand under the shaft.

This is a natural way of holding the club because it feels powerful and it is powerful. That's the trouble. It's too powerful. As you strike the ball the right hand will always overpower the left which is trying to guide the clubhead through the shot.

The player's nails will be facing the sky instead of the direction that the ball should be taking. *This is probably the biggest fault in golf as far as the grip is concerned.*

The outcome of this faulty grip is that the clubhead turns over at impact —mostly producing a low hook. Quite often the player who has fallen into

PLATE 7   This is a weak grip (7A) with the left hand too far underneath the shaft, the right hand too far on top. Both inverted "V's" now point to the left shoulder. As bad, or even worse, is this too strong grip (7B) with left hand showing four knuckles and right hand under the shaft. The "V's" point well beneath the right shoulder.

this kind of grip is unable to use his long woods or long irons efficiently.

If you should have developed this bad habit the cure is to place the right hand more on top of the shaft—as shown in the illustrations of the grip.

What I find when I ask a pupil to make the necessary correction during a lesson is that he invariably tends to "stretch" the right hand over. This starts a chain reaction moving the right shoulder on top too. Which is as bad as the fault he is trying to cure. In effect, he has done nothing.

So remember to place the right hand on the shaft rather than try to "stretch" it over.

All this, of course, is on the assumption you are playing right-handed. Should you be left-handed like Bob Charles then please alter right to left, and vice-versa.

Any change of grip makes the player feel uncomfortable. Not so much at address but halfway through the swing. The cause of the discomfort is that his hands are still trying to work in the old way but cannot.

New movements are coming in which will change the shape of the swing.

But if the player will hit balls for one hour a day for a fortnight using his new grip then I will guarantee that if he reverted to his old grip it would feel as uncomfortable as his new grip did when he changed.

During the transition period life can be difficult and he is likely to hit many bad shots, feeling that he has no control over the club.

Forgetting for the moment the special case of the elderly golfer who is set in his ways, it is definitely worthwhile for the majority of players to suffer for a few weeks and make the change.

The correct grip works well because the palms of the hands are in direct opposition and in a position to operate together as one unit, whereas if the right hand has slipped from the opposing position the two hands can no

PLATE 8   Here's how a friend can help to test how tightly you are gripping.

longer work in unity.

Having learned the correct grip, the next question is how tightly to grip? It is impossible to clasp tightly—vicelike—without the arm muscles tightening too.

Incidentally, I don't like the word "grip" because it sounds vicelike. I would prefer to substitute the word "hold". But since grip is the common expression I shall stick with it.

The club should be held firmly in the hands in such a way that if the clubhead is raised horizontally towards a friend he should be able, using very little force, to roll your fore-arms easily.

At the same time the club should not be slipping in your hands. If the club turns in the hands then the grip is too loose.

But when much pressure is required to turn the fore-arms then your grip is too strong (PLATE 8).

The common fault among week-end golfers is to hold the club too tight. Often they show the whites of their knuckles. Stand on the first tee on competition day and you'll see it.

The player has a psychological feeling that by gripping tight he will give the ball one helluva whack.

It doesn't work that way. By holding too tight he will lose freedom of swing and instead of swinging the club, the club will swing him. It amounts to levering with the club instead of swinging.

There is an exception to the strength-of-grip rule: it comes in the rough when the clubhead is likely to turn over on meeting resistance from the grass.

My advice here is to grip just a little firmer with the left hand—but not the right.

Actually, a loose grip is the lesser of the two evils and is much more likely to be found among lady players. A loose grip can cause the hands to open and the fingers to come away from the shaft at the top of the backswing in what is usually called the "piccolo" grip.

If you have any doubt about the strength of your own grip then get a friend to help and try the clubhead test.

One more thing before leaving the subject of grip. A lot of players think that the golf glove worn on the left hand is one more way for the club professional to grow rich quickly.

Quite honestly a glove does have playing value and I strongly recommend that one be worn. You get a better feel of the club with the master left hand without the grip being too tight.

So having got a grip of the club the next important thing is . . . how do you stand?

CHAPTER THREE

The Importance of Stance

If the grip is a vital part of the game then your stance when addressing the ball is no less essential.

It is important to stand correctly as this will give you balance, a sense of freedom when swinging the club, and, of course, will play a major part in the direction the ball will travel.

There are three ways of standing to the ball—these being square, open, and shut. Many great players have used all three and it is only through trial and error, according to individual build, which one they adopt.

But at the moment I'm thinking in general terms about helping the beginner to get set up for his shot.

With the Square stance, as the word suggests, the feet are parallel to the intended line of flight.

For the Open stance both feet are adjusted to the line of flight with the right foot brought forward about one inch and the left foot taken back a similar distance.

With the Shut (or closed) stance the reverse applies. That is left foot forward and the right foot back from the line of flight (PLATE 9).

I would say that the majority of professionals like to teach a square stance when coaching beginners but I rather favour a *slightly* open stance for all classes of players.

I have found this effective and it seems to work for Mr Average.

Although the feet are slightly open the shoulders are kept square to the line of flight, when using the short and mid irons (wedge to 5-iron). But for long irons and all wood shots have your left shoulder pointing a little right of target. That is to say feet slightly open, shoulders slightly closed.

The reason why I advocate this stance is because most players usually have a habit of turning their hips as far as their shoulders on the backswing.

The slightly open stance helps to stop this as it locks the hips at a 45 degree

PLATE 9 These are the three types of stance—being square (9A) to the line of flight, open (9B), and shut (9C).

turn while still allowing a full 90 degree turn of the shoulders. It also helps the beginner to swing through the ball more freely.

On average your feet should be as wide apart as your shoulders and the toes of both feet should be pointing out a little.

I have noticed that some players, for a reason I cannot explain, get into the habit of turning their left foot as much as 45 degrees. I am not asking you to copy that exaggeration.

The knees should be bent or flexed a little. They must never be locked.

PLATE 10   I posed for this picture to demonstrate the ideal position at address. Points to note are—right shoulder below left, knees a little flexed, inside of right elbow pointing at the onlooker, head behind ball, comfortable and relaxed.

This picture (PLATE 10) shows an ideal stance at address.

The knees are flexed in order to stop tension and because it helps equal weight distribution on both feet.

The weight must never be on the ball of the feet—otherwise you will be tipping forwards too much—but most definitely slightly backwards on the heels.

You should have a comfortable feeling of perfect balance.

Strong legs are essential in golf. On the backswing the body winds up like a spring and with your feet well-anchored it is possible to deliver with the hands maximum power in the hitting area.

If your feet are too wide apart you immediately set up tension in your leg muscles and will find it difficult to turn or pivot when in a slightly bent position.

Should your feet be too close together you will feel insecure. The right distance shouldn't prove much of a problem as most players seem to have no trouble finding the correct width for their stance.

The clubhead should be placed squarely behind the ball—with the hands opposite the ball. This will make them just in front of the clubhead.

The next thing is how far or near to stand to the ball? This distance is naturally governed by the length of the club shaft and the player's build.

But in addition a good guide is to keep your left hand on top of the club. Then the spread span of your four right-hand fingers should be the distance between the top of the club and your upper left leg.

That's an approximation.

Another way is to place your feet together and bend over a little so that your arms are hanging relaxed and pointing at your toes. This will give you some idea as to how far you should bend over at address (PLATE 11).

But be careful not to crouch over the ball, otherwise it throws the whole swing out of true.

PLATE 11   This is a good guide as to how far you should be bending over at address.

The way I teach correct lining up on target is to place a club across the upper chest and shoulders of the player. This indicates exactly where the shoulders are pointing.

I like to find that the club shaft is facing a little right of target. Then having a slightly open stance combined with the shoulders slightly closed (or square) will automatically start the club off on an inside backswing.

You can do this club direction test yourself using the right hand to hold the club across the shoulders once you have taken up your address position.

The right shoulder at address is always lower than the left, the explanation being that the right hand has got to grip the club below the left which automatically pulls the right shoulder down.

The two arms and the club shaft should form a letter "Y" with the right elbow slightly nearer to the body than the left.

I like to see the hands a little down at address.

The head should be behind the ball.

This gives a better view of the back of the ball with the left eye. It also helps to have the head turned slightly away from the direction of the shot.

The business of lining up seems difficult for many players. If a man is knocking the ball to the right he will stand more and more to the left. Or the opposite happens if he is hitting out to the left. In both cases he will be feeding the bad shot and making it worse.

So many golfers line up with their feet which means, since the ball is a distance away from the feet, that the ball will fly to the right.

After many years of playing I line up subconsciously. The way I do it is by placing the clubhead squarely behind the ball and check an imaginary letter "T"—the tail of which is pointing at the target.

The whole composition of the address position must be free of tension and following the procedure I have outlined is one of the best ways to lessen tension. It will further get you set up for an inside backswing.

Grip and stance may seem difficult to the novice but really they are easily acquired and not much of a headache. Nevertheless, they are so important that done wrongly they will throw the whole swing out of tune.

Right, now let's get on to the movements making up the swing.

CHAPTER FOUR

Have a Swinging Time

For the purposes of theory and explaining what happens during the swing, I am forced to break it down into five parts or positions.

I do so very reluctantly since, and I will go more fully into this in another chapter, I believe that the swing should be one continuous flowing movement from A to Z. There are no separate parts.

But we have to know what happens throughout the movement and the best way, even if it wounds my sensibilities, is to take the swing stage by stage.

The trouble is that a little theory can be a dangerous thing. I still chuckle over the serious student of the game who froze at the top of his backswing and complained: "I know how to get it up, but I've forgotten how to get the club down."

Being the opposite of the tired golfer who prayed "Lordy, Lordy, take it up, and I can bring it down."

So far we have got the grip and stance. Now at last we are going to start movement. The swing is a most important part of your game and as the song says "It don't mean a thing if you ain't got that swing."

Here's how to get it.

Assuming you are a new pupil you should feel that you are standing in a barrel with the sides of the barrel two inches clear of your hips all round.

If you bend your knees too much you will get stuck in the barrel . . . so you mustn't do that.

The next thing is that throughout the parts of the swing I am about to outline your body will naturally respond by turning. This is commonly called the pivot.

In theory only and NOT in practice you should not move out of the position you occupy at address. In other words, do the movements I give you without your hips touching the sides of the barrel.

PLATE 12   The five basic stages of the swing. The start (12A) with letter "Y" maintained until almost waist high; waist high to top of swing (12B);

This is possible while making wooden movements but when playing with a flowing swing your hips would touch the sides.

Now what are the positions?

1. From the ball to roughly waist high; 2. From waist high to the top of the backswing; 3. Straight from there back to where the ball would be; 4. From impact to waist high; 5. Finish of the follow-through.

So that you have the various parts clear I have been photographed in each of the stages (PLATE 12).

In theory the top of the backswing of the right-handed player could be recognised as the follow-through of the left-hander, and the follow-through of the right-hander could be the top of the left-hander's backswing.

As you stand to the ball before beginning part one you are in the form of a tripod consisting of your two feet and the clubhead. Your arms and the clubhead should be forming a letter "Y".

the downswing at impact (12C) when, in theory only, you have arrived at an identical position to the address; first half of the follow-through (12D) with the letter "Y" maintained to waist high; and the full finish (12E).

You should be leaning over slightly so that any movement with the club-head will be on an inclined plane—that is to say you will not be swinging parallel with the ground and equally will not be swinging straight up.

Your weight should be evenly distributed.

The letter "Y" must be maintained as long as you can during the back-swing, which means leaving the hands passive while turning the left shoulder under the chin to carry the letter "Y" just past waist level.

In this position the left shoulder will be under the chin, the left knee broken slightly towards the right, and the wrists unbroken. Your head should be stationary throughout.

You are now about to start stage two and you do this by allowing the hands to become a little active. It means breaking the wrists and you will notice that your arms continue on somewhat, and you are then at the so-called top of your backswing.

At this point you should see your left arm straight or practically straight.

But if you find this difficult don't worry too much because we are dealing with an artificial frozen movement.

Your right arm will be bent and your elbow should be pointing at the ground almost like a waiter carrying a tray on his right hand.

If you are of stocky build then not only has your left leg bent fractionally to the right but possibly your heel has left the ground somewhat.

The hands are as high as the top of the head and the club shaft should be pointing along the intended line of flight.

Your shoulders should have turned twice as far as the hips—with the result that the trunk is wound up into a kind of spring.

You should feel that two-thirds of your weight is on the right foot. From here you are in a good position to attack the ball.

Position three is returning the club to the ball. As the hands and clubhead go back to the address position they once again form a letter "Y" on arrival. Which means the wrists will have straightened.

We know that in a full swing the follow-through happens anyway because that is the time it takes to slow the clubhead down to the finish. However, we are practising separate movements so I will explain what takes place.

The first part of the follow-through is exactly the same as the first part of the backswing, but in reverse. The letter "Y" is carried on by the turning of the right shoulder under the chin. This is position four.

You should find that your left leg has straightened and the right leg this time is moving towards the left leg.

All that remains is position five, which is the completion of the swing. Your left arm will be bent in the same way that the right arm bent at the top of the backswing, and the weight should be moved firmly on to the left foot.

The only thing that is different to the position at the top of the backswing is that you should have turned your body completely to face the target, and you will be up on your right toe.

Here is a tip to test whether you have finished in a correct position at the end of your five-part swing. If you swivel your left heel so that the toe points towards the target then you should be in a normal walking position and perfectly balanced.

Again let me emphasise that I hate breaking down a swing into components like this and only do so because there is no other way of passing on basic information. I can hardly wait to move on to the pages where I turn this theory into practice and deal with flowing instead of frozen movement.

My advice regarding practice of the five positions is to run through the first part a few times and then combine 1 with 2, stopping at the end of each position.

Then combine 1, 2 and 3, again with stops, and later add 4. Finally, bring in the last part, by when there will be four distinct stops.

I recommend spending about 15 minutes on the first day just trying position one. The next day spend another 15 minutes combining 1 and 2. Add 3 on the third day's practice, 4 on the fourth, and on the fifth day you can put together the entire swing.

It is important throughout that you keep on checking your grip. With many beginners the grip has a habit of slipping.

You will be using strange muscles and feeling the effects, so it is better to do a little practice often rather than a few long sessions.

Please don't get discouraged by this wooden doll-like practice. It is the hardest part for a new player and quite frankly I sympathise with you should you feel it to be dreary and soul-destroying.

It becomes much easier when you swing the club in one motion but you have to go through this phase and the hardship doesn't last for long.

There are as many swings as there are individuals and in some ways they are like fingerprints. Everybody swings differently although the essentials remain the same.

You may go to four different professionals and likely as not be told four different ways to swing a club. However, there is only one swing and that is a backward and forward swinging of the clubhead.

I never teach anyone a stereotype swing because we all have our own psychology, style, feel, and ability. The player can fit his own pattern once he knows the foundations.

As a young man I made the mistake of trying to copy the swing of the champion of the day, Henry Cotton. The trouble with copying is that you are practising someone else's swing, when it's your own personal swing that will have to stand up to competition pressure.

Practice is the only way to improve. Fortunately, a lot of players find they enjoy a practice knock nearly as much as playing a round. Done intelligently it doesn't have to be a chore.

There are those who think practice to be a waste of time. But it is the best method of getting certain movements ingrained as habit so that they are repeated automatically under match pressure. The muscles remember what they have been taught on the practice ground and respond accordingly when called upon.

Jugglers, pianists, and all those with special skills have to practise continually, and so does the golfer.

You can never say like the confident young girl pupil who had had one lesson: "I won't have to bother again because I learned to play yesterday."

It's about time you hit a ball. Then I shall find out whether you have practised the swing movements long enough.

CHAPTER FIVE

Swing that Clubhead

We've gone through the separate movements and now comes the time to blend them together. What we are seeking is those five parts incorporated in one smooth, flowing movement that we call the swing.

If you have practised diligently then the various parts ought to have become habit forming.

Take the example of a man learning to drive a car. He does it by numbers at first and his movements are awkward. He has trouble thinking about the brakes, the clutch, the rear-view mirror, and his signals. That man is in exactly the same position as the novice golfer.

But once he gains sufficient experience those movements slowly become automatic until he arrives at the stage where he reacts sub-consciously and only thinks about where he wants the car to go. We put the swing together in much the same fashion.

Should you have any doubt about some part of your swing then it is common sense to ask your local professional to check it.

As you put together the five parts into one rhythmic swing I want you to remember that the clubhead is the only part which is going to make contact with the ball.

And during the actual swing you should be thinking of the clubhead and the desired path it should travel rather than the individual parts of the swing with which you started.

However, it is useful to have the basics to fall back on should the need arise.

It will be necessary to swing your club for a while without hitting a ball until the whole blended swing becomes as instinctive as the various parts were in the beginning.

If you are wondering how fast or slow the completed swing should be, I can only reply that the answer differs from pupil to pupil. But taking a mean average—and this particular advice is not original—the ideal swing pace is akin to the tune of The Blue Danube. That's about the pace and rhythm.

What I want to be certain of next is that you have practised the complete swing long enough for it to become so automatic that you will not change it once a ball is placed on the ground to be struck.

I can assure you that most learners definitely alter their practice swing as soon as a ball appears and revert back to natural instincts. The swing they use to hit a ball is nothing like the one they have practised.

This always tells me that there has been insufficient practice on the basics because that is the only way they should know how to swing.

I want you to use an easy club for your first shots, one that is relatively simple to control. Go off to the practice ground with a 6 or 7 iron and give yourself a good lie.

An important point here is the position of the ball between the feet. With these two clubs the beginner should position the ball about two inches left of centre.

Keep in mind that the longer the club, the more the ball is positioned towards the left foot; the shorter the club, the more it tends to move back to the right foot. That's a general guide.

Now I want you to swing through the ball exactly as I have described irrespective of where the ball goes and whether it is a good or bad shot.

I would rather you swing correctly and hit bad shots at the beginning than swing anyhow and hit a good one. You cannot expect this early in your game to hit all good shots, so don't be disappointed by the results.

What you are getting is the feel of hitting a ball combined with the swing.

Or to put it another way: what I am seeking is the swing you have been taught, free and unimpeded, with the ball merely an incident in the swing. It just happens to be in the way of the clubhead as the club moves through.

Don't hit at the ball. You must swing through.

The thing to look for is the ball being sent into the air. Assuming the path of the clubhead to be correct, then if the ball goes to the left or right it is only through the blade being open or closed, and usually it is only a matter of a few degrees either way.

If this happens during your own practice sessions the solution largely rests in your own hands. The more you keep practising, the more your hands will become "educated" and the greater the feel of the clubhead.

To help get the "feel" of whether the blade is open or closed I want you to go over to the putting green for a few putts.

Hit a ball with an open blade and then a closed blade and you will see

PLATE 13 Brian Huggett's swing in X-ray. A first-class example as you might expect from such a player and one thing to note is that the club is still travelling downwards after the ball has been struck.

it travel right and left respectively. You can feel then how the hands affect the squareness of the clubface through the shot.

Next try a number of easy chip shots around the green, say with an 8-iron. Repeat the open and shut face procedure, and then try to hit a few with the blade of the club going through square.

You will be delighted how these little shots will give you the desired "feel" that is so difficult to put into words.

Now you should go through your bag of irons starting with the 9-iron and ending with the 3-iron.

This is a good moment to draw your attention to the X-ray picture of Ryder Cup star, Brian Huggett, playing a 7-iron shot (PLATE 13).

Study the path that the clubhead has taken and imagine you are going to swing your club along the same path.

But there's no need to worry about making body movements because I maintain that if the clubhead path is correct and dominant then all the complicated movements in the swing are a chain reaction to that thought.

And for that reason I am not going to follow the usual policy of harping on such things as weight transference, pulling down from the top with the left hand, right elbow into the side, etc. Those things will happen anyway.

Your swing should be as smooth and rhythmic as the pendulum of a clock swinging backwards and forwards.

In fact, the swinging clock pendulum is the best illustration I know for describing a golf swing.

PLATE 14   The golfer's swing is in many ways just like a clock pendulum and should be as smooth and rhythmical.

PLATE 15   This shows the inclined path of the golf swing and how the clubhead could, as it were, follow the rim of the wheel. Your head being the hub.

If we imagine that our body, like the clock standing on the mantelshelf, is stationary, our arms and club become the pendulum swinging to-and-fro.

As the pendulum moves the bottom of the arc swings over the same spot each time. But if, as the pendulum moves right, you move the body of the clock one inch in the same direction, then the bottom of the arc of the pendulum will move one inch, too.

Equally, if you reverse the procedure, moving the clock back one inch, then the bottom of the arc moves back with it.

It follows from this that throughout the swing your body must remain perfectly still with only the clubhead, hands and arms moving (PLATE 14).

Unlike the clock we cannot swing in an upright plane because we are bending over. This means that we swing on an inclined plane both on the backswing and also the follow-through.

The "wheel" seen in the drawing indicates this inclined plane (PLATE 15).

Again unlike the clock, we have to swing the clubhead further back and through than a pendulum travels, so naturally we have to allow the body to turn on both the back and forward swing.

But I repeat that the feeling is always that of a clock pendulum swinging to-and-fro in a graceful and uninterrupted movement—something you find and admire in the action of great players.

So try to seek similar smoothness.

Do not try to find out how hard you can hit a shot otherwise you are likely to swing yourself off balance. Being able to maintain balance is the reward for good swinging. Much better than trying to hit hard is finding out how to develop greater clubhead speed at impact.

We also have to consider the arc and direction in which the clubhead must be swung.

I have already explained about the inclined plane. Imagine you are addressing the ball: that your head is the hub of a wheel with the rim of the wheel placed around you on an inclined plane, and that the rim of the wheel is groved to allow the clubhead to follow that grove throughout the back and forward swing.

This will keep the clubhead on one even inclined path.

The essential factors you should be getting at this moment of your progress are the feel of the swing, being conscious of the path of the clubhead throughout the swing, and bringing the clubhead back square at impact.

Don't forget, though, that like the clock you must not sway. You're still inside that barrel I wrote about in the previous chapter.

One thing a competent golfer must have is good timing and this can only be obtained if you are fully relaxed. Rhythm is timing and timing is rhythm.

It will help good timing to start your swing quite slowly and gradually build up speed. Then all the moving parts will fit together like cogs. But start swinging too fast and your whole swing will get out of gear.

Next I want to elaborate on the feel of the swing, left side control, and how to keep the body muscles out of the action.

CHAPTER SIX

Hands and Feel

Now that you have been given a swing the fact remains that it is still possible to carry out the movement correctly and miss the ball!

So what's wrong? Your hands are untutored and need educating. And that is what we have to work on here.

Your golf is literally in your hands. Max Bygraves sings that show business needs hands. We golfers need them even more.

After all, it is possible to have a swing looking like a 4-handicap player while at the same time the hands are operating like a 24-handicapper.

There is nothing more important in the golf swing than the hands.

They hold the club, they swing the club, they guide the club and it is through the hands that the clubhead makes contact with the ball.

I have to emphasise that you must try to develop a sense of feel if you are to swing the hands in the correct arc. This sense of feel of the swing is one of the most vital factors in the game.

If you do not believe that the hands are *the* key factor in golf then you are wasting your time following my instruction because that is the basis of my teaching.

The golf swing should be a free swing of the club with the movements of body, arms and legs all secondary and subordinate.

My own experience over the years both as player and coach leaves no room for doubt about the paramount importance of the hands.

Now what is feel? Even Shakespeare would have found it impossible to define. To impart feel is a tough task, rather like trying to describe the taste of certain foods.

It just cannot be done. But when I try to pass it on to a pupil I guide his clubhead in the right arc, thus explaining feel through physical demonstration.

I take him through the backswing, down again to the ball, and right on to the end of the follow-through. I demonstrate it as a complete movement and not as a series of different positions.

That gives some idea of the feel of the swing. It's not perfect but it serves in general terms. After guiding the club a number of times I ask the pupil to try on his own to repeat the example he has been shown.

However, being unable to guide your swing path personally, I can outline another way to acquire the correct and elusive feel that will give you educated hands.

In the previous chapter I mentioned how to make a start to this matter of feel and here is an excellent way to develop it.

What I recommend is standing with feet together, *toes and heels touching*, with the right hand placed behind the back or in a pocket. Swing a 7 or 8-iron with the left hand.

Why the left hand? Because this will get you started on what is called left side control—another significant part of the game which I will come back to shortly. You see me working at this exercise in these pictures (PLATE 16) *see page 56*.

For a change you can use the right hand to swing the club, but do at least three times more swinging with the left hand.

Obviously the best way to retain balance is to place the feet wide apart.

But when the feet are together as shown, any unnecessary body movements, bringing into action unwanted heavy body muscles rather than use of the hands, will at once throw you off balance.

The narrow stance will help you to use the hands correctly with the right feel, and keep out those unwanted muscles.

When my own son, Stewart, was learning to play I made him stay on this exercise for three months.

You can try with or without a ball. Make sure you use the hand on the club fully or it merely becomes a push with the arm. The wrist must be flexed and the hand used to maximum effect.

Heaving at the ball on the course with passive hands only leads to bad shots. The reason being that the strong body muscles have taken over guiding the clubhead so that the hands become secondary and are serving the body instead of the other way round.

I am sure you have heard many golfers say "As soon as I try to hit the ball really hard, I hit a bad shot."

What they mean is that they have exchanged their natural sense of feel and free swing of the clubhead for pure muscle power.

The body cannot do it alone, otherwise a six-foot weight-lifter would be our greatest golfer and people like Gary Player would be better off staying

PLATE 16   The best exercise I know for acquiring feel and building up left side control. With feet together, and right hand out of the way, swing the club freely with the left hand. Have the impression the clubhead is passing your hand as you strike the ball.

in the clubhouse.

If you allow body muscle power to dominate the feel of the hands you will not be playing your best golf. Get the priorities right. It is only good feel that allows muscular power, passing through the hands, to be delivered in the right place in the correct manner.

Your body is like a dynamo supplying power and your hands are the electric wires passing it on.

A poor player who heaves at the ball is using the club more like a lever—and there is no striking force in levering anything. It is the strike within a swing that we are endeavouring to achieve.

When we push in a drawing-pin, that is a form of applied power. But when we drive in a nail with a hammer that is power delivered by striking and exactly what is needed within the swing of a golf club.

I am not asking you to force your swing. Players sometimes say to me "I swung easier this morning, the ball went much farther, and I played better."

They don't realise that what they were getting was the feel. If I want to hit a ball harder then I stand still and thrash with my hands, whereas the amateur throws his body at the ball and recognises force by body heaving.

Actually this causes the clubhead to be slower, moving not much faster than the heaving movement.

The poor player always looks to be straining in every muscle and making a lot of effort in his movement. There is no clubhead speed in this. Only waste of energy and disastrous results.

To keep the body out of the shot the best exercise is once again the feet together position, but this time using both hands on the club.

With the feet together you soon recognise if you are using your body muscles. When swinging with feet together you need good balance, and that means keeping the body still.

All you can really move without getting off balance are the hands, the arms, and the club. There is a little turn of the body but with this exception the body stays perfectly still.

You can go down as far as a 5 or 6-iron doing this practice and should be able to hit the ball nearly as far, if not as far, as when playing a normal shot.

Naturally with the feet together the swing is restricted in length. There are pictures of me doing this exercise (PLATE 17) *see page 58*. I keep going back to feet together practice and assure you that any time you spend at it will pay golfing dividends.

I tell my pupils to keep on practising it until they are sick of it, and then still keep on doing it. There is no finer groundwork.

PLATE 17 Any golfer will benefit from this exercise—the best in the game. It teaches good balance, use of hand action rather than heaving with body muscles, and to do it you have to keep the body still. Another benefit, the greatest of all, is that it helps to give the feel of a swinging motion.

When you come to swing with feet apart you will maintain the same feel as with feet together and will be swinging the clubhead with the hands, with the other movements following automatically.

Left side control that I mentioned is important because while for most people the right side is the strongest and most dominating, in golf the left side must control the swing.

The right side is always trying to take command. *Right side domination is the most common fault in golf.*

You have got to bring the left side alive in order to produce left-hand control.

The exercise I have just described will help and you should make a point of using your left hand and arm as much as possible about the course.

I do so, even to the extent of pulling my trolley with my left hand. Subconsciously while passing time I always swing a club with my left hand.

My friend Jimmy Adams is a firm advocate of left-hand exercise and told me: "My own method when I want to get sharp is to hit balls into a net with the left hand only for two weeks. Which in turn gives control to my left side.

"It revives muscular memory. For an amateur out of training I believe it will take him about two months of practice to get his left side control, but it is essential to a good swing.

"People like Neil Coles, Ben Hogan and Peter Thomson are at an advantage because they are naturally left-handed although playing right-handed.

"Hogan was so poor as a boy that he couldn't afford to buy left-handed clubs so had to play with the right-handed clubs he had been given."

This is as far as I can go without getting too technical in the matter of feel, keeping heavy body muscles out of the swing, and becoming left side conscious.

Once again there is no short cut. Regular practice on correct lines is the requisite.

Having studied the grip, stance, swing movements, and the feel of the swing, we can now advance to the use of the various clubs on the course, hitting off with the short irons.

CHAPTER SEVEN

The Irons

We're learning the clubs now. Most books of instruction start off with the driver but I believe it is better to learn to walk before you run so I am beginning with the short irons and working up to the driver.

Most players are more confident using the short irons rather than the power clubs because they are easier to control.

I wondered for a while whether to include the No 7-iron along with the 8 and 9 clubs in the short irons but feel that maybe it belongs more to the mid-iron range.

In my view a golfer who cannot play his irons, in particular his short irons, is beaten before he goes on the course.

An approach shot to the stick is a vital part of the game and if you can use your short irons with precision you will make up any deficiencies there might be in some other part of your play.

You must not try to overdo distance obtained by an 8- or 9-iron. Bear in mind that these clubs are for accuracy and that *a three-quarter shot with them is recognised as a full shot.*

In this picture (PLATE 18) you can see Roberto de Vicenzo's three-quarter backswing.

I don't want to find you swinging the club round your neck. That's wrong.

Obey one golden rule and you won't go far wrong. And the rule is *the shorter the club, the shorter the swing, and the narrower the stance.*

With the short irons the angle between the clubhead and the shaft is more acute than with longer clubs. This means, along with a shorter shaft, that you are standing closer to the ball and more upright.

This will automatically give you a more upright swing.

I want you to feel that you are swinging all clubs, irons and woods, in the same way but that the differences which result are built into the club.

PLATE 18 That ever popular South American champion, Roberto De Vicenzo, shows his ideal version of a three-quarter backswing.

Take the two extremes: The driver produces a flatter swing and the 9-iron a more upright swing. But that happens through club design and you should believe in your mind that your swing has been the same throughout.

Don't consciously develop one swing for an iron and another for a wood.

Where do you use the 8 and 9? You can use the 8-iron when popping at the green from 100 to 120 yards, while the 9-iron is perfect for around 80 to 100 yards. (Any yardage given for a club is mean average only and will vary from player to player.)

But let's treat these two clubs alike for the purposes of instruction and get set up to play a typical shot.

You're on the fairway, the green is beckoning, and you have selected your short iron.

Try to imagine a line from the ball to the target and have your feet slightly open to that line—which will mean the left toe two-or-three inches back from the right. The shoulders are square to the intended line of flight and the ball is positioned a little bit back from the centre of your stance. Say an inch or so. This alters according to the individual and physique.

A little bit back from centre means the ball will be hit a more descending blow which will produce maximum backspin.

What we are seeking is a rising shot coupled with strong forward thrust rather than a high-flying ball.

If you hit the same ball from left of centre, that is positioning it forward towards the front foot, then you will get a higher-flying shot.

Move it back towards the right heel and you will experience more of a low-flying driven shot. This is used by the experts for control when playing into a strong wind.

But forget this for the present. It is something for the more advanced player.

Through positioning the ball slightly back of centre for the routine stroke you will be hitting the ball down and through before the bottom of your swing arc is reached.

This will result in a divot being taken after the ball has been struck. The divot coming where the bottom of the arc would be.

So the clubhead is still going down when the ball is being struck.

A warning here: don't overdo it. Otherwise the result will be a chop and you will find the divot being taken before the ball instead of after.

Whereas taking a divot after the ball is essential to crisp iron play.

It is a firm shot requiring little body movement. The action involves the arms and hands. There is a slight easing of the knees, but all movements are naturally much less than when using the longer clubs.

The wrists will cock early in the backswing but there is no need to try to bring this about consciously. It happens anyway.

The hands will be a little ahead of the club blade at impact.

When you practice always have a target in mind and never strike off blindly. Vary your distance from time to time because nobody can tell you how hard to hit your shots for a given distance and this will help to teach you judgment of the power required.

It is better when approaching a green to hit a firm shot with a reduced swing rather than taking the same length swing as for the longer shot and hitting easy.

Shortening your swing will produce a short crisp shot. And short and crisp is preferable to long and easy.

There will be occasions at some short holes when the 8 or 9 can be used off the tee.

Don't become a victim of pride and merely drop the ball on to the turf, or adopt the habit of knocking up a piece of ground for a make-shift tee.

The game is difficult enough without adding to the difficulties. Should you have a chance to tee the ball then do so. It will help you get the ball into the air.

Having said which, make sure you tee close to the ground. If you make the mistake of teeing too high there is a danger of hitting the ball with the top of the blade.

The biggest problem with the short irons for beginners is that having taken a lofted club and wanting to see the ball fly high, they fall into the trap of trying to help the loft of the club by scooping.

The result is usually either a topped ball or the ball hit very heavy—turf before ball.

You must always trust the loft of the club and be confident that if you hit the back of the ball correctly then the club will send the ball into the air without help.

A good tip when playing to the green is to get into the habit of aiming for the top of the flagstick. So many players aim for the bottom of the pin and invariably end up short. It is better to be past the hole than short.

With regard to weight distribution on the shot, I wouldn't worry too much about this yet. But when setting up have the impression that the weight is evenly distributed on both feet.

This helps to give balance and keep the body out of the shot.

Finally, the 8 and 9 clubs are also used for pitch shots—as opposed to full approach shots—to the green. For this type of pitch shot the feet are closer together, the stance more open, and the swing must be unhurried.

Hand and arms are very active and the clubhead must be kept along the intended line of flight.

The short irons are most useful to any player anxious to reduce his handicap. If used well they can leave you close enough to the hole to single putt.

Try to get to know them well because they are stroke savers from fairway or rough and you will be calling on them frequently during any round of golf. It's a good thing, by the way, to practice from the rough and other trouble spots so that you are prepared when you get into trouble on a proper round. Use these clubs to attack the flag and master them to the extent that you rarely miss a green with them. No championship has ever been won by a player lacking in this department.

If you watch the tournament professionals you will find that they rely on the clubface to get the ball up and never try to scoop the ball into the air with unnecessary and faulty hand action.

I think you will find that judgment of distance rather than faulty use of the club is likely to prove your biggest headache.

THE MID IRONS

I am calling the 5-, 6- and 7-irons the mid irons. These should present no great problem as the faces are lofted enough to get the ball into the air and inspire confidence.

In fact, I would say that with most novice players the 5-iron is their favourite club.

Depending upon individual capabilities the range of these three clubs ought to be in the 120 to 150 yards bracket. You might get 165 yards out of a 5-iron but I am thinking in average terms.

These clubs are often used off the tee at short par three holes, while on the longer holes they are used for hitting the green. A word of warning: the bigger the club the greater the possible margin of error.

Don't hesitate to use these clubs out of the semi-rough, only remember that in the semi-rough grass will come between the clubhead and the ball.

This reduces backspin and the ball is likely to have a lot of run. So don't expect it to hit the green and stop dead.

You will probably get greater distance out of the semi-rough than off the fairway due to this fact.

And if the grass is wet you could get what we call "flyers"—that is the grass acts almost as grease and the ball slides on the club face. When that happens you could send the ball out of control and as much as 30 yards longer than normally allowed for the club.

The only way to obtain this kind of knowledge is through experience.

Anyway, if you are playing out of semi-rough you are asking a lot to expect target golf results.

Otherwise it is the routine mid iron fairway shot that we are really considering.

The mid irons have longer shafts than the short irons, which means you will be standing farther away from the ball. They are also slightly flatter in lie and with the degrees of loft reduced.

I would still adopt a slightly open stance as for the short irons, and once again the weight is evenly distributed. The stance being slightly wider.

For the 7-iron shot the ball should be central between the feet, moving the ball towards the left heel no more than one inch for the 6-iron, and certainly no more than 2 inches from centre for the 5-iron.

Some players, Peter Thomson for one, prefer to use all three clubs from the same centre position.

We place the ball more or less centre in order to produce a descending blow which will bring into play the loft of the club. This in turn gives backspin and increased driving force.

Where you get backspin you find height coupled with control and the ball biting and stopping quickly. These are the essentials for all iron play.

Now that we are getting to the longer distance clubs lining up on target becomes more difficult. I think it will help you to feel that your left shoulder, which will be higher than the right, is pointing directly at the flagstick.

Check that while your feet are in an open position your shoulders have stayed square to the desired line of flight.

At address the hands are opposite the ball. The arms are taken away in a one-piece movement, maintaining for a foot or so the letter "Y" formed by the arms and the club shaft.

Then the hands become active, producing the natural wrist break.

As with the other irons the ball is struck first, turf after. There is a kind of squeezing effect involving the blade and the turf.

You should be seeking a clean, decisive blow and not the sweep of a wooden club. The clubhead in taking a divot goes on and through the ball.

Take a look at the 5-iron shot I am playing (PLATE 19) *see page 66 and 67.*

By now your swing is upright and long enough to bring in the danger of the right shoulder getting into the shot at impact. This is that most common fault, right side domination, which I have already mentioned.

You've swung across the ball and it goes straight to the left, or with the same shoulder-fault shot with the face open, the ball will fly straight with slice, or to the left with slice.

So make sure the clubhead arrives at the ball before the shoulder and that you are facing square to the ball at the time of striking.

The 5-iron is most useful when playing into a very strong wind when the club that would normally be used for the distance is a 7- or 8-iron.

This particular shot is played by holding the 5-iron down the shaft a fraction and keeping the clubhead low to the ground on the backswing. The face is slightly shut and, with a short backswing, give the ball a firm driving punch with scarcely any wrist action. Keep the clubhead close to the ground on the follow-through.

Then the ball will stay low and under the wind.

All three mid irons can be utilised round the green when playing gentle run-up shots.

You want to imagine you are using your putter, with the difference that it is a putter with loft. I find this the easiest way to tackle the run-up shot.

Make a point of having your weight on the left foot and the hands ahead of the ball.

There is another occasion when the 5-iron proves a valuable club. That is when you are unfortunate enough to find your ball resting in a divot mark

E

PLATE 19   In this sequence of pictures where I am playing a 5-iron
shot you will notice that the positions are almost identical to those

in the fairway and you need to play a long shot.

The drill is to position the ball right of centre—which results in quite a
descending blow. What you are doing is turning the 5-iron into a 4- or 3-
iron, but with the advantage of having a shorter shaft.

THE LONG IRONS

I have played against many of the greatest names in world golf and
watched at close quarters many others of the tournament circuit stars, yet
the finest long iron player I have ever seen was someone hardly anyone will
know.

He was the Egyptian professional, the late Hassan Hassanein. I played
with him when he won the Italian Championship at Villa d'Este close by
Lake Como.

What was so impressive about his long iron skill? He was an absolute
wizard with a No 2-iron and hit the ball a phenomenal distance without
any effort. Yes, he was very, very long.

seen in the feet-together pictures. As I'm only interested in flowing movement I won't discuss these positions "frozen" by the camera.

I wonder if this was due to the fact that as a boy in Egypt he played golf without shoes which meant he had to stand completely still for fear of slipping and played more with his hands and arms, with little hip turn. But he did have an excellent shoulder turn.

There is no doubt that the stillness of his body made him such a superb iron player. The nearest to him among present-day players is the legendary Sam Snead.

I noticed in Hassan's action that he played very flat-footed and only came up off his right foot well after completion of his shot.

What am I trying to get at here? The lesson is that although he had a bigger club in his hands he didn't hit any harder than his hands and arms would allow, and was able to keep out of the shot those unwanted body muscles.

He was anchored with his flat stance—this position being the first cousin to the feet together exercise that I was extolling earlier.

The long irons are the Numbers 1, 2, 3 and 4. Although if you are Tony

Jacklin winning the British Open Championship then you use a No 1-iron which has been converted to what he told me he calls a Zero iron.

However, we can forget the Zero and 1 iron quickly. Over many years as a club professional I don't suppose I have been asked to supply nine or ten 1 irons.

The reason is simple: I would say that not one amateur in several hundred is able to use it successfully. Usually those who were keen to try the club wanted it as a substitute for a driver which was giving them trouble off the tee.

They wanted to try something different but after experimenting most were prepared to admit defeat. Nevertheless, some of the pros use the 1 iron most effectively off the tee and from the fairway.

On the assumption though that I'm dealing with ordinary mortals, well, the 1 iron has no part in your game.

Which leaves us with Nos 2, 3 and 4.

The 2-iron is also a specialist club and I love using it myself. But my own experience with week-end golfers is that not more than one in twenty wants this club included in his bag.

It is used for accuracy and distance from the tee when a driver seems inadvisable, and used correctly the 2-iron is a more accurate club than the No 1 wood.

I use it off the fairways on a seaside course when the ground is sun-baked and the ball is getting a lot of run. You can manoeuvre a 2 iron with greater chance of success than a 1 or 2 wood.

It is especially useful into the wind and if you know how to play the shot will keep the ball low and driving forward after it has landed. It also lessens the risk of an unkind bounce from a high ball.

The 2 iron is probably not so attractive in wet conditions when the fairways are soft. In those circumstances there is more likelihood of getting better distance from a wood shot.

You can use a 2 iron off the tee at the long par three holes and, varying slightly with the conditions, ought to be thinking of getting around 190 to 230 yards out of the club.

Some professionals can actually pitch a green with a 2 iron and stop the ball quickly. But again this is something outside the scope of Mr Average.

Like the 3-iron it has special use when the ball is in trouble and the next shot has to be kept low under tree branches, etc. Always assuming that the lie isn't too tight, the 2 iron, with so little loft, will tend to keep the ball low.

But it is this very fact that makes it so difficult for many handicap players to use it with confidence.

PLATE 20   Gary Player seen in action off the first tee during the British Open Championship. His 4-iron finish is exemplary. He is well balanced and the right shoulder is immediately over his left toe. The hands are right through the shot and high.

The 3-iron is the average player's long iron and this is the club that sets generally start with. The chances are this is the longest iron you will be able to wield successfully.

You will be calling on it for long fairway shots to the green. But because of the distance involved—approximately 190 to 210 yards—don't imagine that you are going to achieve perfection and rule your ball down the stick consistently. Still, given time and practice that is the ultimate.

The club is correctly and frequently used on the long par three holes and off the tee at "tight" holes where it would be dangerous to risk a wood.

A typical example would be when you are aiming down a tree-lined fairway or when you fear a wood shot would reach a cross-ditch or bunkers.

It makes sense to play short of the trouble with the 3-iron, while at the same time you will still be covering a lot of ground.

Never use it in the rough and only sometimes in the semi-rough when the ball is lying nicely. Even then it must not be forced. The rule being if in doubt about the lie, forget this club.

It can also be used from just off the fringe of the green when a minimum of loft is required to set the ball off on its way.

The 4-iron is the favourite among the long irons with most players. It has a good average length shaft with a reasonable degree of loft, and can be counted on to send the ball up to 200 yards in suitable conditions.

It is a club for using off the tee, off the fairway, out of light rough, and for the fringe of green shot just mentioned.

The 4-iron is distinctly useful and I suggest it is the first club of the long irons you should try to master (PLATE 20) *see page 69.*

Next we'll consider the positioning of the ball—assuming you are starting with the 4-iron.

The ball should be closer to your left foot. Say about one-third of the way between the centre of your stance and your left foot.

For the 2- and 3-irons the ball moves still proportionately further forward towards the left foot. About $2\frac{1}{2}$ inches inside the left heel would be perfect for the 2-iron.

Some instructors advocate that all iron shots should be played off the centre but I find the best results come by moving it more to the left side.

The weight is a little more on the right foot, in the proportion of what

PLATE 21   My address position when using a long iron. Open stance and right shoulder back and out of the way.

PLATE 22   I am using a long iron in this shot and a backswing of this length will suit most players. A three-quarter swing helps control.

seems to me to be 60:40. This brings the right shoulder well below the left.

The stance should be slightly open with the left shoulder aiming a little right of target. Now what we are after is a shot that comes down, under and through.

I find that most players have a habit of tensing up at address with these longer clubs, so it is essential that you help to reduce tension by flexing your knees a trifle.

At address your right elbow should be slightly bent and in towards your right side, with the left arm and club shaft being almost in a straight line (PLATE 21).

You are coming into a bigger swing and the wrist break arrives later, just before the hands have reached waist level. The club must be taken back with the clubhead low to the ground.

By doing this you will take advantage of the loft coming into the ball.

It is a common fallacy that because the player is using a longer club he thinks he has to have a longer swing.

What I like to see is just past a three-quarter swing and certainly not past horizontal. Curb any tendency to sway or the feeling that you must put more into the shot because you want the ball to travel a long way.

Rely on hand and arm action as I assure you they can produce all the power required (PLATE 22).

The commonest fault with the long irons is the slice. Usually caused by coming into the ball too late. Which means the hands are way in front of the clubhead at impact.

This produces an open blade and a cutting across action.

What I am giving next is an over-correction but it works. *I want you to feel when you practise that the clubhead is going to reach the ball before the hands.*

Even if you seem to be achieving this, the near certainty is that your hands and the clubhead are arriving together.

There are two irons still to be mentioned and these are the wedge and the sand iron. They are clubs apart and for that reason merit a chapter to themselves.

Before that, though, I think we can get out the woods.

CHAPTER EIGHT

The Woods

When considering the woods, and leaving aside the driver to be the subject of the next chapter, we are really dealing with the Numbers 2, 3 and 4. These are the commonplace woods and their function is for distance.

I have known a player who carried a bag full of woods, from driver to 8 wood, in preference to irons. The explanation being that this chap socketed with his irons all the time.

But he's rather like that rare individual who prefers a three-wheel to a two-wheel bicycle.

I am told that there is also a No 9 wood around. If there is, I haven't seen it.

What I must not exclude, though, is the high-lofted No 5 wood which has been introduced in recent years and earned increasing popularity—in particular among the older players, and most definitely with the ladies.

The No 5 wood is really bringing back the old-fashioned baffie, which had more of a rounded sole, in a modern form.

Some players use it as a substitute for a 3 or 4 iron because the large head gives them more confidence and they can get the ball into the air with less effort.

The 5 wood can be used off the tee at short holes and is most useful for getting the ball out of a tight lie in the semi-rough when an iron would be inadvisable. It is also possible to get tight lies on the fairway, and here again you can call upon the club.

I am frequently asked by people who buy a 5 wood what iron it is intended to replace. In all honesty I find that impossible to answer.

The 5 wood is sure to send the ball high and, taking the two extremes, against the wind could be the equivalent of a 6 iron, while with a following wind could pitch as far as a 2 wood.

I recommend the club to the average woman player and to anyone having difficulty getting the ball into the air with his long irons.

It is the kind of club that is going to "drop" the ball to ground. By which I mean the ball is going to run out of steam quickly.

Let me make it clear that I am by no means suggesting everyone should carry a 5 wood.

The most popular of the woods is the No 4. It is an easy club to use, has a nice small compact head, is well weighted, and has a generous loft. It is an interesting fact that it has more loft than a 3 iron.

The 4 wood is a versatile club with a multitude of uses and should prove one of the most active clubs in your bag.

You can drive with it, use it off the fairway in wet-or-dry conditions, take it in semi-rough where—unlike the iron—it will spread the grass rather than cut . . . a real utility club.

But you have to be careful playing against the wind, as it has its limitations.

I have played in many tournaments and gone out armed in the way of woods only with a driver and the No 4. However, I can easily turn the 4 into a 3 wood and when playing against the wind could always take out a 2 iron for preference.

You can manoeuvre the 4 wood and I am sure that the vast army of golfers wouldn't dream of going out without the club in their set.

The good player once he is on the fairway uses it to hammer the ball towards the green. But there is more error than with an iron shot, and it is also harder to make a wood shot hold on the green, due to the fact that it produces less backspin than an iron.

Under normal conditions a 4 wood shot should be between 190 to 230 yards.

The 3 wood is slightly larger in the head and with less loft. Many handicap players are quite content to drive their way around the course with it, as they find they have a better chance of getting the ball straight down the middle.

Rather reluctantly they will accept the fact that it also means they are going to lose some distance against the wind.

Still they gain in confidence and direction and prefer to accept the penalty rather than chance the more difficult 1 and 2 woods.

As most handicap golfers hit the ball too late anyway, the loft of the 3 wood is somewhat diminished and without knowing it they are really turning it into a 2 wood (PLATE 23) *see page 74.*

Personally I think of the present-day 3 wood as a power fairway club, even if Peter Thomson won a British Championship driving with his 3 wood

PLATE 23   For the fairway woods the ball is positioned left side of centre. The stance is wider than with the irons, and the weight is noticeably behind the ball at impact and just after.

at most holes.

If I am going to leave any clubs out of my bag then I drop the 2 and 3 woods.

When newcomers to the game come to select their clubs I know from experience that the vast majority, if they are buying half a set, prefer to have the 2 and 4 woods rather than the 1 and 3. The ratio is as high as 25 to 1.

I find that the 3 wood is used more frequently than any other wood at the longer "short" holes where a strong shot to the green is necessary.

As a rough guide, when we take out the 3 wood we should be thinking of 230 yards maximum.

In using it from the fairway the average player will require a fair lie.

If it is not a fair lie and 3 wood distance is wanted then I advise settling for a 4 wood instead.

One of the recurring problems with the club among amateurs is that, as they are invariably aiming at a distant green which is heavily protected or in a corner close to or out of bounds, they wonder whether to play short with an iron and settle for safety.

When that poser is put to me I reply that winners are usually players who attack the flagstick and I like to see all my pupils optimistic.

Obviously there are times, according to circumstances, when safety first is a golden rule. But if it is just a friendly four-ball match then I like to see everyone giving it a go.

You will never win a championship by playing defensively over four rounds. Intelligent defensive golf has its place, but you will not get in a position to use it unless you have been playing attacking golf at other holes (PLATE 24) *see page 76.*

The 2 wood or brassie is designed for the maximum distance you can get off the fairway. It is *the* power fairway club. Never use it unless the lie is very good and even then resist the temptation to try to force a few more yards from it.

Distance? Think in terms of 210 to 240 yards.

While designed for the fairway the 2 wood is most commonly used as a driver off the tee. Quite often professionals do so when they have a tight fairway to hit.

I recall playing with Bobby Locke and he said he used his 2 wood off the tee for 5 or 6 holes at the start of any round "until my eye is in."

I think the reason the 2 wood is a favourite with many players is that the extra loft can be seen when addressing the ball and along with a feeling of confidence it allows a greater margin of error.

PLATE 24   Jack Nicklaus winding up for a fairway shot playing the long 11th at Lytham St. Annes. He has a wide backswing and note his left foot is flat on the ground which will help to stop his hips turning too much.

Which is no doubt why, generalising, the ordinary amateur likes to drive with his 2 wood and take his 4 wood for the long second shot.

Psychology comes into this. I am thinking of the man who doesn't want to drive with a 2 wood in case he is thought inferior, yet doesn't want a No 1 wood because he knows he is unable to use it.

Noticing this problem some years ago I am sure I was one of the people who prodded the manufacturers into making a 1½ wood. This is really a No 2 wood with 1½ on the bottom.

But it allows the man to put a No 1 headcover on his wood and save his pride.

To prove the part psychology plays I can mention a customer I once had who complained that his new 2 wood sent his drives too high.

Knowing in my own mind that he could not use a driver I suggested he should have a 1½ wood. All I did was take his 2 wood to my workshop and change the sole plate to one stamped 1½.

He came back after trying it out and said how pleased he was to be keeping the ball down! He went away delighted.

In windy conditions, when the wind is behind, I find that a fairway 3 wood is just as good as a 2 wood, sometimes even better.

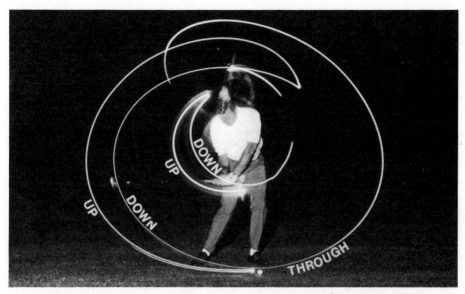

PLATE 25   An X-ray of long hitting Ryder Cup player Peter Alliss. The path the clubhead has taken is perfect and the line thinning close to impact shows that clubhead speed is at its greatest then.

Against the wind, though, there is a marked difference in favour of the 2 wood. Off the tee even if the wind is behind you should still go for the 2 wood.

In playing your 2, 3, 4 and 5 woods there is no need to vary the position for each club whether the shot be off the tee or from the fairway.

The ball is positioned about two inches inside the left heel. The stance is slightly open with the line through the shoulders pointing just right of target. This stance and lining up will vary fractionally with the individual.

The feet must be wider apart than for the long irons and the old maxim about having them as wide apart as the shoulders applies for these clubs.

With all woods the swing is somewhat slower and longer. Having the feet wider apart helps to preserve balance. Another good thing is to have the toes turned slightly out.

A lot of people disagree with me on this but I would have the weight just a little on the back foot at address with your left shoulder riding high.

All long hitters have their weight on the right foot at address and even momentarily at impact.

Knees are flexed to cut out tension and make sure you stand up to the

PLATE 26   Comedian Jimmy Tarbuck, mid-handicap player, has a good action but seems to come off the ball very soon.

ball with your left arm and club shaft almost in a straight line. The right elbow is bent a little.

Avoid any tendency to crouch over the ball as this will alter your swing and get you hitting the ground before the ball. At the same time it is equally bad to get into the habit of reaching for the ball.

A wide swing is essential. Study this X-ray of Peter Alliss (PLATE 25) *see page 77* which Frank Sowerby took at Coombe Hill when he and I went to comedian Jimmy Tarbuck's house.

This is the kind of swing path we are seeking. The clubhead is low on the backswing and stays low to the ground after the ball has been struck.

As an interesting comparison to a top pro swing I have included an X-ray of Jimmy Tarbuck, who like so many in show business is a great golf enthusiast and a useful handicap competitor.

The Liverpool Lad is low on his backswing but comes off the ball too soon—that is the clubhead leaves the ground too soon after impact.

Otherwise he's got quite a nice action.

On a wood shot the wrists break later in the backswing, so maintaining a wide arc, and don't actually break to their maximum until the player is on his way back to the ball.

This gives the illusion as shown in the photograph (PLATE 26) that he is hitting too late. Ideally you will finish with your hands in a high position.

The follow-through with all clubs is most important. Every time you swing try to hold your follow-through for a second or two. You should be able to do this while still maintaining your balance.

The way you follow-through is the result of the way you attack the ball at impact.

The prime fault with the woods without any argument is caused through heaving. The player wants to obtain maximum distance and not satisfied with the yardage he can get with his hands, brings his body into the shot.

Before leaving the woods I am amazed how many players don't appreciate that the woods are lighter than the irons. And the lightest club of all?

That's the Big Boomer. The driver. The club we're coming on to.

CHAPTER NINE

The Driver

The driver is the glamour club of the bag and some players get their golfing satisfaction purely from the distance they can hammer the ball rather than from their final score.

We all know the run-of-the-mill player who loves to boast about how far he has knocked the ball off the tee. I have to admit there are times when I have to stop myself from asking if he knows in which direction it is going.

In a major tournament you usually find that the title has gone to the man who combines good driving with razor-sharp putting.

First-class driving off the tee will not only demoralise your opponent but will make your own golf easier. If the ball finishes down the middle and has travelled a fair distance then afterwards you are playing what amounts to a series of short holes all the way round the course.

The exception being, of course, those two or three long par-five holes which may be out of reach in two wood shots.

Which leads one automatically to the story of the Irish caddy who told his player "Sure, into this strong wind it'll need three good shots to be up in two!"

If I had to choose between accuracy with my driver or long hitting I would go for accuracy every time. Obviously accuracy combined with distance is the ideal.

Think about this: Club player "A" considers himself a big hitter and on the first tee booms one down the fairway for 280 yards. He skies his next drive which goes 190 yards, and his third drive he tops to register a measly 120 yards. This gives a total yardage for the three shots of 590.

Meanwhile, his opponent, player "B", being a consistently steady but unspectacular golfer, is driving them down the middle 230 yards every time. Making his total 690 yards.

So in actual fact player "B" is the longer hitter on average although

PLATE 27 My right shoulder is well down in this picture of a typical driving position. The ball is positioned up to two inches inside the left heel. It may look more central here but that is due to the camera angle.

player "A" will be remembering his own opening drive.

Most golfers will tell you instantly that they find the driver the most difficult club of all to use. I think a lot of it is psychological.

They are unable to see much of the face of the club and this breeds anxiety. Also because they instinctively think the ball should be hit a long way they try to give it a tremendous thrash.

In so doing they exchange hand movement for body muscles.

Another factor is that any slight degree of error in driving is magnified by the distance the ball is going to travel.

Personally, I cannot understand why most players find the club so hard to use. In theory it should be the easiest.

You are playing from even ground and the ball can be teed up to any height which means everything is in your favour. Nevertheless, the fact remains that mentally it is the club which produces most concern.

The driver I use myself is the one I recommend to others. It has a deep face and a liberal degree of loft—this aids confidence—and is not too heavy.

The first thing with any drive is to tee the ball correctly. I like to see the middle of the ball level with the top of the club face at address—as in PLATE 27.

F

That's another generalisation and I am well aware that some champions tee still higher while others tee barely off the ground. But follow my guidance and you won't go far wrong.

Take up your stance with the ball positioned 1-to-2 inches inside the left heel. The reason for this being that the clubhead will then reach the ball just after passing the lowest point of your swing arc.

Which means it will connect as the upswing is starting.

Once again I advocate a slightly open stance (that is, for a reminder, left foot a little behind the right) with the shoulders slightly closed.

The feet are slightly open because this will help you to turn after the ball has been struck, while having the shoulders slightly shut will start you off on an inside path on the backswing.

Should you find you prefer to take up a square stance, with shoulders and feet both parallel, then by all means do so. There is very little between the two positions and I only prefer the first because experience has taught me that it suits most people and gets the best results.

It is so easy to tighten up while using the driver—and so important to try to relax.

A relaxed feeling is best achieved by having a practice swing, flexing the knees, and not taking a stranglehold grip on the club. The good player will also introduce a short waggle or two in preparing himself for the strike.

Your feet should be placed about as wide apart as the shoulders, the hands are opposite the ball, the right shoulder will automatically be lower than the left, the right elbow is flexed in towards the body, and the left arm is dominating (PLATE 27).

So far as the head is concerned feel that the left cheek of your face is behind the ball.

The actual swing is the same as with your other clubs. But this is only in the mind as since the driver shaft is longer and you are standing further away the swing becomes flatter.

However, the club does that on its own and there is no need to make any conscious adjustment.

I have to emphasise how important it is for the feet to be firmly anchored. You have only to try hitting a ball while standing on an icy surface or a muddy tee to realise the importance of a firm base.

Power requires a firm anchorage and if you haven't got it then it becomes almost impossible to play a powerful, accurate shot. The boa constrictor has to have some anchor before squeezing its prey to death so it wraps its tail round a tree or some similar object.

If it doesn't have an anchor then it is unable to supply power. The same holds true for the golfer.

Let me set down some Do's and Don'ts for the driver—and these also apply, perhaps in lesser degree, to your other clubs.

PLATE 28   American tournament winner George Archer, who stands 6ft. 5ins., is seen playing in a championship. He has a wide swing and has hit well past his chin. His right foot is flat on the ground showing that his weight was well behind the ball at impact.

PLATE 29   I am on the way back to the ball. But notice that my wrists are still well under the shaft. You can almost feel the power.

DO remember, and this is vital, to keep your head completely still throughout the entire swing. The head will move forward after you have hit the ball but by then the ball is well on its way. Keeping the head still also helps to stop any dipping action (PLATE 28).

DO take your time in getting set up correctly. This is most important.

DO swing the club back through a wide arc preserving the letter "Y" of the arms and club shaft for as long as possible. This will result in the club-head being taken back low to the ground.

DO feel at impact that your left shoulder is "sliding" as it were up the flagstick. This way the right shoulder comes down and under your chin; at the same time you will find your right knee kicking in towards your left.

DO take your time on the backswing. You can only hit the ball on the down swing and the whole process is a gradual building up of power and speed.

DO try to limit the length of your backswing. Certainly not going further than having the club shaft parallel to the ground. At the same time the shaft should be pointing along the intended line of flight.

DO have in mind to sweep the ball off the top of the peg rather than using brute force.

DO check that both wrists are well under the shaft at the top of the backswing (PLATE 29) *see page 83.*

DO keep the club face looking at the ball for as long as possible when starting the backswing. This makes it easier getting the club back square at impact.

DO try to have the right arm straight soon after impact as this will give you width through the ball keeping the clubhead low longer after the stroke (PLATE 30).

DO work towards a full finish with the hands high, the shoulders square to target, and balanced on your left foot—with shoulder, hip and knee immediately over your left toes (PLATE 31).

Now for the Don'ts . . .

DON'T sway. If you keep your head still then this cannot happen as it's impossible to move your body and leave your head behind.

DON'T throw the clubhead from the top otherwise maximum clubhead speed will be spent before the ball is hit.

DON'T be too anxious to look up and see where the ball has gone. Better to remember "head still".

DON'T flick or snatch at the ball through trying to gain extra power at the last moment. Clubhead speed must be built up gradually from the top of the backswing.

DON'T throw your body into the shot in the search for increased distance. This is what mostly causes loss of balance.

DON'T shut the face of the club on the backswing. If you do so, and it is a common fault, then you have to make compensating adjustments to return the clubhead square to the ball. Two wrongs can make a right in golf but simplicity is the sure path to consistency.

PLATE 30   Here's what I mean by right arm straight soon after impact.

PLATE 31   Tony Jacklin is almost at a full finish on his way to winning his first Open Championship. It's a real champion's action.

In summarising, the biggest fault with the driver is that too many golfers want to throw their whole body at the ball.

This is their way of recognising power. But you have only to see the small, slightly built man outdriving Mr Atlas to know the real secret of power:

STAND STILL AND DELIVER THE POWER GENERATED BY THE BODY THROUGH THE HANDS.

There is an old-fashioned idea that the right elbow must be tucked into the side at the top of the backswing to the extent that it has been possible to swing with a handkerchief held tight under the armpit.

Don't fall for it. More often than not it produces a very open clubface at the top of a backswing.

The idea was fine in the days of hickory shaft and gutty ball when the problem was getting that sort of ball into the air. Now with today's clubs we have more trouble keeping the modern ball down.

Some instructors still teach the handkerchief tip. Sorry, but its day has gone.

But enough of power. As a change we can pass on to finesse. Which means taking a close look at the use of the wedge and the sand iron.

CHAPTER TEN

On the Beach

I used to be a terrible bunker shot player and, in relation to the rest of my game, will admit to being the world's worst. The change came when I was twenty-six and played with Harry Weetman in a challenge match against Bobby Locke and Max Faulkner.

During that round I suppose I was in four sand traps. Each time I managed to get out but the shots were so bad that at tea time Bobby Locke, a supreme golfer and four times British Open Champion, came up to me and said: "You should make the Ryder Cup team in a couple of years but the worst thing in your game is your bunker play."

He asked if I would mind if he gave me a tip or two.

He left his tea half-eaten and took me out to the bunker at the 18th green and demonstrated 12 to 15 shots putting the ball all round the stick.

Then he had me in the trap playing shots and showed very simply where I was going wrong. It was so easy and I can still see that picture.

It was through fright at being in a bunker that I developed anxiety and tried to play the shot as quickly as possible in order to get the suspense over.

This meant that all my movements were fast. He stayed for half-an-hour getting me to swing the club so slowly that I felt the club was hardly moving at all.

From that moment on I can honestly say I have been a good bunker player, and I still am.

Today I would rather be in a sand trap alongside the green than having to chip over a bunker.

So my trouble was due to a fear complex. But this fright on seeing the ball in a bunker is a common malady among week-end golfers.

Some of the antics they perform to get out are laughable and some, especially women, even play out backwards.

Believe me there is no great difficulty involved in getting out of sand.

A bunker shot round the green under ordinary conditions is one of the easiest shots of all.

In view of my own personal one-time bunker fears I have great sympathy with golfers who say they find the shot terrifying.

If you are one of them I offer the consoling thought that with bunker play there is a greater margin for error than with any other stroke.

You never come in contact with the ball during an explosion shot close to the green. Hit behind the ball $\frac{1}{2}$ an inch, 1 inch, or 2 inches, and it will come out.

Equally true, though, is that it may be nowhere near the flag.

Take a look at any modern sand iron—or exploder. It has a very enlarged flanged and rounded sole, which helps to stop the club from digging too deep into the sand.

This means that the shot is much easier to play than in the old days when they used a club known as a niblick. That would be roughly the same as today's 9-iron.

The sand iron is an essential club and I advise you strongly to carry one in your bag. By the way, it is the heaviest club of them all.

As for bunker shots, there are two distinct types: these are (1) the explosion shot used mainly from bunkers around the green, and (2) the fairway bunker shot when distance is needed in addition to getting the ball out of the trap.

Let me begin with the greenside explosion stroke. When taking your stance make sure you adopt a very open position with the ball opposite your left heel.

The purpose of this is to make the ball rise quickly.

Keep the face of the club square to the line of flight and when you swing do so with the swing of the club parallel to the line of the feet.

This produces an out-to-in swing which results in a steepish backswing and the wrists cocking a little sooner.

In taking up your stance shuffle your feet about in the sand to obtain a firm foothold, at the same time learning from this action whether the sand is soft or hard.

Remember that the rules of the game do not allow the clubhead to touch a grain of sand before your stroke has been played. So make sure you keep the clubhead slightly above the sand at address and during your backswing, otherwise penalty is incurred. Of course, you can touch the sand when actually striking the ball.

You have to decide for yourself how much sand to take—which means how far to hit the ball—and only experience over a period of time can teach you this.

The amount of sand you take will determine how far the ball travels.

Anyway, forget those bunker blues and tell yourself that the explosion or splash shot is one of the easiest to play.

You address the ball with your hands opposite your left knee, which means they will be ahead of the ball. This automatically opens the clubface slightly.

The explosion swing must be long, slow and deliberate. Little force is really required. The follow-through is an essential part of the stroke so never leave, like so many players, the clubhead in the sand.

If you stop on the shot it will be 10 to 1 the ball will stay in the bunker.

Most occasions you should be hitting about 1 to 1½ inches behind the ball and should have a feeling of almost dragging the clubhead through the sand.

Don't forget though to keep the stroke going and make sure you hit well past your chin.

Another thing to remember when entering the hitting area is to make sure your right elbow is into your side. This will ensure that the hands stay well in front and help keep the clubface to the sky for a while.

It is mainly a hands-and-arms shot apart from the natural pivot. The

PLATE 33 Even Jack Nicklaus has to practise! This time he is showing how to play a difficult bunker explosion shot.

PLATE 32   These are two perfect bunker shots being played by Peter Alliss and Bernard Hunt. Their clubhead lines are almost identical.

wrists cock almost at once on the backswing but never really fully uncock on going through the ball.

Never roll the wrists. This is sometimes called pronating. Rolling the wrists could start you on the dreaded shanking.

Keep your hands low to the shot, which means fairly close to the knees (PLATE 32). These are first-class explosion shots played by Ryder Cup men Peter Alliss and Bernard Hunt which say the lot about bunker technique.

When you see such a perfectly played shot the ball rises quite steeply, sand is sprayed around the area, and the ball drops like a poached egg and either stops dead or screws back (PLATE 33) *see page 89*.

The cardinal sin with a bunker shot is to take a short backswing and try to pick the ball cleanly off the top of the sand.

This might seem to be the natural way but it's an illusion. Even the experts are wary of attempting this disastrous shot.

Another fault is scooping and trying to help the loft of the club.

With the fairway bunker shot where distance is desirable—imagine you have driven into a bunker which is 200 to 250 yards from the green—the

club you take is determined by the height of the bunker face and how near your ball is to it.

The stance is the same as for any normal iron shot (which means slightly open), the difference being that the ball can be positioned a little closer forward to the left foot.

Decide what club you feel you can clear the bunker face with. If you settle for a 6-iron then take a 7 or 8. It's better to be back on the fairway than playing your third shot from the sand.

Make certain you hit the ball first and take it cleanly. You must not hit the sand first.

Should the lie be exceptionally good and the bunker shallow, with the ball fairly well back, then you can take a 4-wood. There is some degree of risk but you are taking a reasonable gamble.

The golden rule is to get out whatever happens and get the ball back in play. This may mean on occasions even settling for an explosion shot when the conditions are tough.

There is what I would describe as a kind of halfway bunker-shot—halfway between the greenside and fairway bunker strokes.

I'm thinking of the bunker placed about 75 to 80 yards from the green and with probably another bunker to clear at the edge of the green.

Take it from me this is the hardest stroke in golf. Precise judgment and striking are required here.

The way to play it is to take up your stance as though about to play a 9-iron, but using a sand iron or wedge. The object is to strike the ball first, taking sand afterwards.

By doing this you have a good chance of sending the ball the desired distance. Don't be too ambitious with this stroke. Settle for the middle of the green rather than fancy pin-splitting.

Should you find your ball in a deep bunker then it must be played more off the left side.

The difficulty comes because whereas on turf you can get away with an indifferent stroke, should you hit sand first the stroke is deadened through the sand forming a cushion between the clubface and the ball.

Obviously there are a number of "headache" problems found generally with any kind of bunker shot. For example, the ball is resting in a heel mark or is buried in its own pitch mark.

Play a slow and deliberate explosion shot, except you will need to use more force than usual. In addressing the ball you should even open the clubface a little bit further. Also take a firmer grip with the left hand.

From a shallow and lipless bunker alongside the green there will be rare occasions when it is common sense to play out with a putter. Experience will teach you how hard to strike.

Try to hit halfway up the ball so that the putter never comes in contact with the sand at all. It is a stiff wrist action.

When the greenside sand is wet or hard, and seaside bunkers are liable to pack, then your sand iron with its heavy sole will bounce off.

You don't want that so choose instead a sharp-edged iron, probably a 9-iron. Still hit behind the ball and the club will bite into the sand.

When your ball is buried in the rising face of the bunker it is often impossible to play forward. You must settle for a sideways or backwards shot.

Remember the guiding factor: get out at all costs. You have made a mistake going into the bunker in the first place so be prepared to accept a one-stroke bill.

When the ball has just rolled into a bunker and is touching the edge (which means a chopping action is the only one possible) then try to take turf first.

This stroke requires considerable force. After which you can only hope and pray.

Then there are those deep wall-of-death bunkers, and the Old Course at St. Andrews comes to mind where some bunkers are almost as upright as the wall of a house.

To get out of these you play the ball right off your left toe, open the club face considerably, cut across the ball from out-to-in, and use plenty of strength.

CHAPTER ELEVEN

The Wedge

Like the sand iron the wedge is a special club and you must spend some time becoming really competent with it. I make that point because the wedge has so many uses.

But while it is versatile it is basically designed for delicate pitch shots to the green when a lot of backspin is required, also for short approach shots ranging up to about 100 yards.

You can also pull out the wedge on the shorter short par-three holes— say up to 120 yards if the wind is favourable.

PLATE 34 America's big money-winner Billy Casper sometimes finds the rough. Here he is using a wedge out of deep rough. Note the firm hold.

In addition, though, to these pin-splitting strokes it comes into play when escaping from thick rough, hitting shots over trees, for tight or scraped lies near the green, and for scrambling shots off stony paths (PLATE 34).

The wedge is designed on similar lines to the sand iron and has a heavy flanged sole. But where the sand iron has a rounded sole with the back higher than the leading edge, the pitching wedge has a flat sole and the blade is usually on the square side.

First I want to run through the main shot that the wedge is called upon to play and that, as mentioned, is an accurate pitch to the pin with maximum backspin.

Your stance should be very open and narrow. As this is the shortest club in your bag, involving quite an upright swing, it means you will be standing much closer to the ball.

You play the ball from about the centre of your feet, with hands opposite the ball and shoulders square to the line of flight.

From this position you will discover that your backswing is quite steep and your wrists break much earlier than on other shots.

This steep swing, which incidentally must not be too long, results in a descending blow which in turn brings about the desired backspin—the ball either stopping as it lands or sometimes pitching and coming back.

The harder the surface you are playing from the more backspin will be imparted by the ball being pinched between the clubface and turf.

Make sure you carry through to a good three-quarter finish and it is most important, as with other shots, that you finish the swing with a firm grip.

When playing the wedge make sure you have your weight at address evenly distributed on both feet. There is very little foot action. The left foot should stay firm on the ground during the backswing because this curtails any unnecessary body movement.

Even though the backswing is quite upright it must still be made inside the line of flight. And make sure at the top of the backswing that you are looking at the ball directly over your left shoulder.

On returning to the ball keep your wrists cocked for as long as possible—it's not length we're seeking but accuracy. Then hit the ball first and take turf afterwards.

A useful tip is to feel at some stage in your follow-through, say halfway, that the clubhead is pointing at the flagstick.

I want you to practise with the wedge. Practise a lot with it. Make a start from different positions around the practice green.

The wedge is worth getting to know since it is such a stroke saver. Put the effort in and this club can become your best friend.

But if you think it is a club that will play itself, needing little attention, then it can be your worst enemy. The wedge in the hands of great players is a sight worth seeing.

Here are some faults to avoid:

When using it to play over a bunker never try to help the loft by scooping

PLATE 35   This is what you mustn't do. I'm scooping at the ball and trying to help the loft of the club. Any number of club golfers fall into this trap.

PLATE 36   But here is how the shot should be played, leaving the loft of the wedge to take the ball into the air.

(PLATE 35). That is your hands stop but the clubhead goes on with the left hand collapsing at impact.

All you produce then is a fluff or the ball skimming across the green half-topped and out of control. The wedge has enough loft built in and doesn't need your help to do the job.

Don't stand too far away from the ball, as this will bring about a flat swing when the club is meant to be swung upright. With these two opposing factors you are in danger of shanking.

Never use the wedge with a sloppy hand action. What you want is a short, firm swing.

If you want to play a low wedge shot then move the ball more towards your right foot, close the clubface, and have the hands almost opposite your left knee. Take a shorter swing and pinch the ball between clubface and ground.

Played properly this is a useful shot around the greens. You will notice the ball skid up to the pin, trying to stop on each bounce and very controlled.

The opposite is wanting the ball to fly high. For this the ball is positioned opposite your left heel with the face slightly open and the hands level with your left knee. Make certain you swing right through the shot.

When you find yourself in some thickish rough around the green with no obstacles in front then you are forced to accept that only a scrambling shot is effective.

What you do is grip the club well down the shaft, at the same time positioning the ball between your feet. Swing the club quite steeply and chop down on the ball with little or no follow-through.

This will squirt it out low and the ball should be on the green somewhere. The only guide as to how hard to chop for varying distances is practice. You must also take into consideration the thickness of the grass or heather in which the ball is sitting.

When using the wedge it is necessary to have good touch. A delicate but firm action is called for and I am sorry to say that precision with this shot has eluded me all my life. You can be certain I have tried all the methods in the world.

You may find equal difficulty. In which case why not consider the action for which I have settled? It gives a good success average.

I have reduced my hand action to the minimum by playing the stroke stiff wristed. I feel that I am swinging the club from my shoulders and say to myself on the backswing "Left shoulder under the chin," on the through swing, "Right shoulder under the chin" (PLATE 36).

All the while feeling that my hands are passive. I know of course at the back of my mind that my hands are controlling the club but I have cut the action down.

I feel that if I could have had the touch with the wedge, and I'm sure it is inherent, I would have had a better tournament record. The more I think of it the more convinced I am that the delicate touch of wedge play is something you are born with—or without.

G

One man who has the gift is very strong and hits the ball a country mile. I refer to Harry Weetman, who has represented Britain many times.

Despite his strength when around the green and using his wedge he has the sensitive touch of the surgeon.

The first three fingers of the left hand are the key ones in this shot. Keep the left hand guiding and keep the clubhead going through.

So many players become anxious halfway through their stroke and let the right hand take over control. This brings about a scooping action.

If this is one of your faults the way to stop it is to overlap two fingers of the right hand instead of one.

It takes much of the power away from the right hand and gives increased feel with the left.

Go to work on your wedge because if you can pitch and putt well you will take a lot of beating.

CHAPTER TWELVE

The Art of Putting

Is putting really bracketed with the game of golf or is it a game within a game?

I have heard many arguments on this subject and I know that some of my fellow professionals maintain that it is a game apart.

They say that the putt is not a golf stroke.

Where we all agree, though, is that putting in the tournament circuit game is what makes the difference between high and low scores.

Hence the saying "You drive for show and putt for dough."

Shortly before he won the British Open Championship I had the opportunity not only to X-ray Tony Jacklin's swing but also to help him with his putting.

I asked him to imagine he was trying to hole a 25-footer—and here you see the result (PLATE 37) *see page 100.*

You will note that the line of the putter head finishes about knee high. This caught my attention at once as we have always been taught to keep the putter blade close to the ground.

I pointed this out to Tony and he replied that it could be the reason why he had not been holing so many of his long putts.

I asked him to try another 25-footer, this time keeping his putter closer to the ground after striking the ball. The result was better but to my mind still not close enough.

For comparison the X-ray picture I have of Ryder Cup player George Will shows a dead-straight hand line, whereas Tony's hand line is half moon (PLATE 38) *see page 101.*

If you think of a par 72 course, allowing two putts for each green, then half the strokes are played with a putter.

This, of course, would be a perfect round of golf. It may be rare but it happens.

PLATE 37   Not a good action this time. Tony Jacklin is playing a 30-foot putt and the X-ray shows the putter head and hands finished much too high. Also his head has moved with the ball.

Even if you three putt some greens and single putt an equal number of others you won't need an accountant to realise that overall you have two-putted.

But these are the days of sub-par golf and the top men will break no records with a 36-putts-a-round average. Now the target must be somewhere between 28-32 putts per round.

No matter how advanced your capabilities, you are going to miss some of the greens with your approach shots. Which means you must get down with a chip and one putt.

Yes, putting is the only way to really low scoring.

This holds true for every class of golfer.

And nobody knows it more than the week-end golfer who was four-putting every green and eventually in desperation turned to his caddy and implored "What is the secret of putting?"

The caddy thought about it for a moment then said "Try to lay your second putt stone dead."

Here's something to think about: most courses are over 18 holes and the usual course includes four par-three short holes.

PLATE 38· Good action by George Will on along putt. The hand line is straight, the clubhead stays low to the ground, and his head stays still.

Providing you get threes at each of these, you can miss with your second shot the remaining fourteen. But get down from off the green with a pitch and one putt and you will be round in 68.

This seems easy but you have to be a good putter to achieve it. So let's see if we can improve your performance.

In general terms there are three categories of putters. Not the Good, the Bad and the Ugly, but the Good, the Inconsistent, and the Poor.

This last individual would have trouble sinking his ball in a dustbin lid.

Before delving into putting theory and practice let me raise the matter of equipment. With the good putter there is no need to offer advice. He could sink 'em with an upturned walking stick.

For the other two categories I recommend the centre-shafted putter as being worth a trial. I think it lessens striking errors and provides added confidence.

Choosing the right type of putter is a very personal matter, as we all have our likes and dislikes. What is essential is that every putter must have a little loft. This helps the ball to start straight.

Without going to the extreme of choosing something too heavy, a putter

PLATE 39   This is the putting stance I recommend. Weight on left foot and both hands well under the shaft.

with a little weight is easier to control than a light one. You can feel the head better.

Right, now let's get down to sinking the ball.

Your feet should be wide-enough apart to allow you to keep your body still, and the ball should be inside your left foot—up to four inches inside the toe (PLATE 39).

I believe a lot of players make a mistake in the distance they stand from the ball. I cannot provide a definite yardstick, since it depends on how tall you are and whether you have an upright or flat putter.

What should be avoided, however, is taking up a position which, drawing a line from your eyes to the ground, is directly over the ball or, worse still, outside it.

If you do this you are looking at the far side of the ball while at the same time trying to hit it along the intended line (PLATE 40).

This creates difficulties and will invariably send the ball left. A much better position is to have the line from the eyes slightly inside the ball.

Find out which is your strongest eye by lining up a finger with a distant object with both eyes open. Then close one eye at a time.

The master eye is the one which still sees the finger lined up with the

PLATE 40 These two pictures show the wrong and right way of standing to the ball. In the first I am too far over the ball but the second position is ideal and makes it easier to line up the putt.

object. With the weaker eye it will be well out of line. When putting you should be looking at the back of the ball with your master eye.

Naturally your head will tilt one way or the other, depending upon which eye you are using.

I am not suggesting by this that you should have one eye closed when you actually putt, but concentrate on getting the master eye focused on the back of the ball.

If you favour Arnold Palmer's famous knock-kneed stance there's nothing against that. The value of his particular stance is that it locks the body against movement.

Any individual stance which passes that vital test is suitable.

It's also good to have your knees gently flexed and the weight slightly on your heels and your left side. This gives a feeling of anchorage more than anything else.

The putter grip is definitely different from the other clubs. You can have your palms opposing but this tends to make the elbows spread out, which

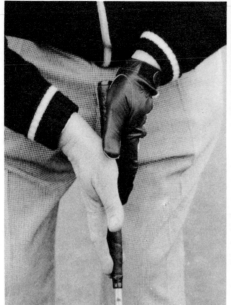 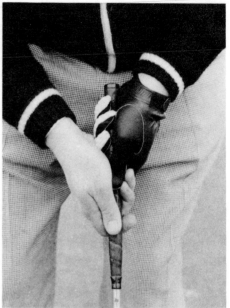

PLATE 41   If in taking up your putter grip you have the two palms opposing like this then your elbows will be sticking out. Not recommended.

PLATE 42   A good orthodox putting grip with the hands at the back of the shaft and the elbows into the side.

can create looseness in the stroke (PLATE 41)

I think the best type of grip is to move the hands fractionally off the front of the shaft and slightly round the back (PLATE 42). You will note straight away that the elbows close into the sides.

Some people use the reverse overlap grip—that is forefinger of the left hand overlapping the little finger of the right. This is good because putting is really a right-handed game.

I'm not saying that you must adopt a similar grip. In fact, I prefer the ordinary overlapping style.

As to the stroke, as I explained at the start of the chapter, it is most important to keep the blade close to the ground throughout.

Some people putt with a very wristy action, which can lead to inconsistency. Stiff-wristed putters are usually more repetitive, but best of all is a combination of these two methods. I think the combination is less chancy and definitely makes it easier to get the feel of distance.

You can push, tap or stroke a putt. I don't favour the first two actions and will explain why.

If you push a putt along it means you are holding the putter too tight and it can make your whole body move. If it is overdone you can actually hit the ball twice.

In tapping the ball it is almost impossible to judge distance, especially on long putts. On short putts you will sometimes get away with it.

The stroked putt gives a feel for distance and makes the ball roll straight off the club. It keeps rolling over the grass without bouncing so much.

Incidentally, if you have ever judged a green to be slow and given the ball a sharp rap only to finish well past the hole, the likely reason is that the ball has jumped off the blade and doesn't start to roll until it is well on its way across the green.

We know that to hit a longer ball it is necessary to swing the putter farther back. To get the right distance the important factor is how far you swing the blade through.

Take the example of trying to toss a ball into a basket. The greater the distance the more your arm will go through but it doesn't necessarily go farther back to achieve the greater distance.

When I'm teaching I tell my pupils to get the feel that they are throwing the ball with their right hand towards the hole. It provides a sense of feel and direction.

Obviously, practice is essential. I find a good way of judging distance in practice is to draw lines at suitable intervals—say at 3, 5, 7 and 9 yards (PLATE 43) *see page 106*.

Putt at these lines alternately ball by ball. Try to finish on the line *or just past*. Never up, never in.

Something else I have found very good is to sink a tin smaller than a golf cup into the ground and putt into that. Do it long enough and the real hole will look that much bigger.

Like so much else in the game, experience is the great teacher when attempting to read greens.

On reaching the green you should be checking the slope of the whole green itself, and within that the little burrows themselves.

I always get down behind the ball for the final lining up. If you're not sure then walk to the other side of the hole and look back to the ball. Also look at your putt from the side.

Once you have decided how far to the right or left you are going to hit it—and the strength—come what may you must stick to that line.

Don't get frightened half-way through your swing and hit it a little more

PLATE 43 A useful way of judging the strength of a putt.

left or right.

With the uphill putt you have to decide something for yourself which could be an exception to the "never up, never in" cliché.

You obviously have to strike the ball harder and the danger is that going too far may leave a dangerous putt coming back down the slope. It's not a bad time to settle for lagging up. But it's a personal decision.

Because the ball has been struck firmer it usually sticks to the uphill line and will not break so readily to the side.

With the downhill putt, decidedly more difficult, the ball has to be be trickled and is much more susceptible to the putting surface. Again "lagging up" is advisable.

The curly two-footer? I think on average you will hole more by hitting firm and straight than by finesse.

If you can master putting it will help make your chip shots less anxious. But if you are a poor putter it can affect your whole game. You are always tense trying to pitch up right alongside the stick to avoid any danger of three-putting.

We all have our own pet gimmicks and characteristics. Far be it from me to pass judgment on them. If they give you help and confidence, that is all that really matters.

However, I would ask you to remember that "a missed putt is never a missed putt until it is past the hole." Finally, a word of advice should the dreaded putting "yips" ruin your game. The nerves at the ends of your fingers are very sensitive so make sure you hold the putter more in the palms of the hands. It is one possible way to tackle this uncontrollable curse.

CHAPTER THIRTEEN

The Common Faults

After a routine round of golf there is always one shot, but never more than two, that the ordinary player will look back on and say that he played to perfection.

In which context it is interesting to note that whereas the club amateur will drop in at the pro's shop and talk about his good shots, the tournament professional will prefer to talk about and analyse his few bad shots.

The amateur enjoys his momentary triumphs whereas the pro, who has become accustomed to a degree of near perfection, expects all his shots to be first-class and is disappointed when he fails for some reason to maintain his own high standards.

For both tiger or rabbit disaster is always lurking round every corner of every course. In a way this is a good thing. It keeps us on our toes and stops even the greatest player from becoming too confident.

You may have wondered why it is that some "boy wonder" players seemingly set for stardom suddenly fall away either in their late teens or early adult life.

I can think of a number of well-known players who were written up as world beaters of the future who never fulfilled their promise.

What invariably happens is that these brilliant young lads were gifted enough to play their golf instinctively and automatically. Results start to flow at once and their confidence is immense.

Perhaps it is over-confidence but invariably at this point in their short career—and I would ask some of the excellent young players coming along to remember this—their game suffers a setback.

One or other of the common faults I am about to tackle creeps into their game.

For these future stars it is a black moment when their golfing confidence and invincibility are dented and from looking like potential golfing geniuses they start to appear mere mortals.

This is a vital moment. They either have to seek advice or work out a solution for themselves. It means going back to the basics and it is only if they can live through this period, and it could last for two or three years, that they will get back on the victory trail once again.

By then, of course, very much wiser and knowing a whole lot more about their own game.

Possibly the most consistent British tournament player is Neil Coles. While still a young man, and fortunately before he had tasted great success, he ran into trouble with fading the ball.

He spent one whole year ironing out the fault with my assistance and during that time never entered a single competition. That took tremendous will power on his part.

We all, amateur or professional, have one particular bad shot which consciously or subconsciously we have to guard against. It is never far from our mind on the course.

I used to suffer with a fade—but knowing your weakness does bring along compensating factors and keep a healthy check on over-confidence.

I believe that we can learn from our mistakes. Some experts say you should never tell a player the reasons he has made a bad shot. Better to concentrate instead on giving him positive advice.

My own contention is that the player has to know why he has played a bad shot in order to understand the cure. A good teacher goes deep and finds out the cause of a poor movement.

All of which leads me to this list of common faults in stroke making. The terrors of golf.

I don't care how old the man may be or how long he has been playing and ingraining a particular fault, if he is prepared to co-operate I promise that he can be cured of any of these prevalent faults.

As golfers we are seeking perfection. Which is unobtainable. So don't be frightened of your errors, because I am certain that every star name in the record books has experienced at one time or another every one of these faults.

What we have to do is learn why they happen and how they can be corrected. I am setting down the usual reasons followed by some successful remedies. The illustration (PLATE 44) *see page 110* will prove helpful.

THE SLICE. Without any doubt this is the No 1 malady and the explanation is simplicity itself. It so happens that the natural way to hit a golf ball is conducive to a slice.

A slice occurs when the clubhead is swung across the ball from right to

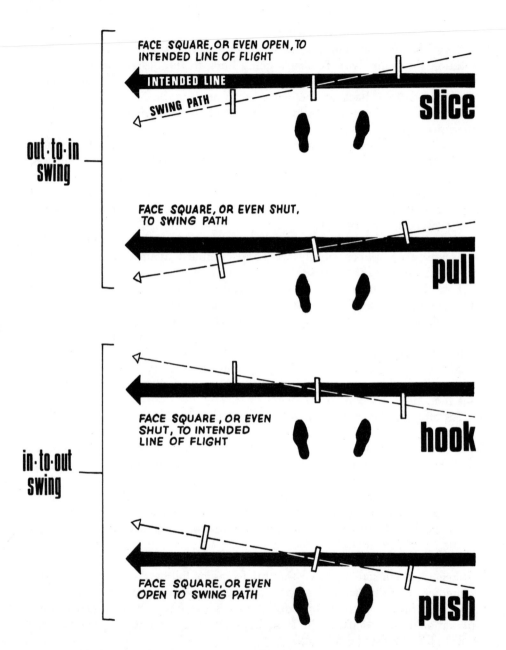

PLATE 44 Slice—pull—hook—push.

left with the club face open. This gives the ball a glancing blow, which imparts clockwise spin and sends the ball first to the left and then curling away to the right.

This has involved what is known throughout the game as an out-to-in swing. The thrust of the clubhead is sufficient to start the ball off to the left, and, as momentum lessens, the spin takes over and curls the ball to the right.

The reason why a natural swing produces the slice is that as the club returns to the ball the left side turns out of the way. Regrettably, the shoulders turn along with the hips.

Obviously since the copybook golf swing is going against nature this fault is the most difficult to cure. You could say that about 90 per cent of players slice somewhere or other while playing their normal golf.

One main cause is that the player gets his hands and body into the shot too soon, which results in the clubhead coming in *too late*. The clubhead slides across the ball.

Some points which help: see that your stance is not too wide, start the clubhead on an inside path, and try from the top of your backswing to get the clubhead to the ball first.

There are two common forms of slice: (A) That's the one I've already described and (B) one where the ball starts straight and then turns right.

While slice A may get fair results because the ball often finishes in the middle of the fairway after flying down the left-hand edge, take it from me that it is the worst kind.

Slice B is caused by the clubhead coming into the ball along the line of flight, but with the club face *open* at impact. Had the club face been square the ball would have travelled straight.

Should slice B prove your trouble then the open face could be the result of a weak grip; face open at the top of the backswing; or hands too far ahead of the ball at impact.

Weak grip in this instance means, looking down on your hands, that the inverted "V"s of your left and right hands are pointing at your left shoulder instead of your right (PLATE 45) *see page 112.*

However, as already indicated, it is slice A which gives much more cause for concern.

The first thing to check here is the line of the backswing. Make certain the clubhead is not going back outside the line of flight, also that it is not being picked up too steeply from the ball.

This not only gives you a bad position at the top but brings about a chopping strike as well.

PLATE 45 Roberto De Vicenzo won't be slicing this wood shot. He's reached a good position at the top with the clubface square.

Try to ensure that your left shoulder and the clubhead start to turn on the backswing together, and that your right elbow at the top of the swing is pointing to the ground. Your right wrist ought to be underneath the shaft at this stage.

In starting the backswing feel that the clubhead stays looking at the ball for as long as possible, remembering it's a turn we're after and not a sway.

The next thing is to return the club to the ball without throwing the right shoulder into the shot. This should give an inside-to-out path to the clubhead.

If you find it difficult keeping the right shoulder out, and you may, feel as you approach the hitting area that your hands are going to brush past your right-hand trouser pocket.

I can also give you three "over-correction" hints if you continue to have difficulty keeping that right shoulder under control:

(1) Try to hit the ball while your back is still facing the target.

(2) Try to hit the ball keeping your right shoulder behind your head.

(3) Get a golf ball box and put it under your left heel. Now try to hit the ball without crushing the box. This helps to stop you turning too soon.

Some instructors advocate a closed stance as the cure for a slice but I think this only aggravates the basic problem.

When you visit the practice field always make a point of practising from the left-hand corner, at the same time feeling that you are aiming up the left-hand side.

Instinctively this should make you want to hit the ball away from you to the safety of the right. In other words, swinging inside-to-out. This is the movement you are after.

Never practise trying to cure a slice with the wind at your back, as this will have the effect of making you turn into the ball even more.

One more never . . . never aim off to the left to neutralise your slice, as this will only make it worse.

Feel you are swinging round on the backswing and away going through. As you swing you can say to yourself "Round and away".

THE PULL. This is exactly the same swing as for the slice, the only difference being that the clubhead has returned to the ball square. The ball moves in a straight line to the left with no side spin. Once more it's an out-to-in swing.

Should the club face be closed at impact then the ball will fly to the left but hooking at the end of flight.

The same remedies apply as for the slice.

THE HOOK. This is the exact opposite to the slice but you are over-doing correct movements. Hence the saying that anyone can slice but it takes a golfer to hook.

The hook is a scything action.

The ball starts to the right with anti-clockwise spin and turns sharply to the left.

It can be caused by a flat backswing which generally leads to the club returning to the ball too much on the inside; a too strong grip, that is the right hand too far under the shaft; closed club face at top of backswing or at impact; or even too steep a backswing—which has the player looping inside the line of the backswing.

It is an easy business curing the hook.

Check through the causes I have listed. Swinging flat isn't really a common fault. More often than not it is the grip which can be blamed.

The right hand has slipped under the shaft with the inverted "V" now pointing outside the right shoulder, or the left hand has gone too far over showing three-and-a-half to four knuckles.

Closing the club face during the backswing is caused by the wrists turning under.

Mostly I find hooking occurs when the left hand collapses at impact and the right hand takes over, so closing the face. The antidote is to take a little firmer grip with the left hand.

THE PUSH. As the pull goes with the slice, so the push is the same swing as the hook. The ball travels straight to the right.

It is caused by the same things as the hook except that the club face is square to the line it is travelling on.

To correct a push make sure the clubhead is looking squarely to the ball a little longer on the backswing. Check your grip to see it is not in a weak position with the right hand too far on the top of the shaft, and the left hand too far under.

Check that your body is not too far ahead of the ball at impact, or that at address the ball isn't positioned too much right of centre.

TOPPING THE BALL. If a ball has no backspin it will not fly. So a topped ball is one hit above centre, imparting so-called top spin. It will travel in the direction it is struck but never leave the ground.

I have heard many times that when a ball runs a long way after landing "it was hit with top spin". There is no such thing as top spin. What we do have is maximum and minimum backspin. If it was struck with top spin it would never become airborne.

Topping is fairly common among beginners. Closely associated is the "thinned" or half-topped ball.

There are people who say topping is caused by "head up" or looking up too soon. Keeping your eye on the ball during the swing helps, although it is still possible to be looking at the ball and top a shot.

This happens because your body comes up or stretches up and raises the arc of the swing.

Topping is mainly caused by swaying into the shot either on backswing or downswing. Whatever the cause the arc of the swing has been raised.

Other causes are snatching, scooping, or having the arms bent just prior to the strike.

The solution is to stand still throughout the swing and make sure there is no swaying movement. Don't stoop too much at address, and feel you have stayed behind the ball at impact. A good tip is to try to strike the ball along the ground. You will find it impossible to do—except with a putter.

THE SKIED SHOT. This happens when the ball is hit well above centre of the club face. The ball balloons into the air and flies high rather than long.

It's not all that common and relatively easy to clear up.

The general cause is that the player has picked the clubhead up too steeply—picks it up, that is, instead of swinging it back.

As a result he reaches a steep chopping position at the top of his back-swing and the club descends on the ball too sharply.

What we are seeking is a low striking action, and allowing the loft of the club to take the ball into the air.

The remedy is to keep the clubhead low to the ground going back, brushing the turf. Also check that you do not have too much weight on your left foot at the top of the backswing, and that you do not roll your wrists before impact. Incidentally, there is a misconception about wrist roll. It's the forearms that roll. But we still talk about wrist roll.

THE HEAVY SHOT. You get this when you take turf before hitting the ball. The ball doesn't travel far as the power of the shot has been cush-ioned by the turf.

The cause can be the same as for the skied ball, except that you may even be swinging steeper still. A tendency to scoop can contribute, or hitting from the top of the backswing so that the clubhead is well ahead of the hands at the strike.

The cures are the same as for the skied ball: keep the clubhead low to the ground on the backswing, maintaining the same even path, and make sure you don't dip or sway.

THE SHANK. Some players regard this as the mystery shot of golf. Others say it is psychological . . . and up to a point it is.

You can be playing a perfect round of golf when without warning you hit this dreaded shot. If you have never experienced this terrifying moment then count yourself lucky.

The ball flies off at right angles to the player and on examining the club you will find a ball mark has appeared at the heel of the club.

The most common clubs with which it occurs are 7-8-9-irons, the wedge, and the sand iron. You can shank with all irons but the short irons are the most suspect. It's a disease which can strike from beginner to tournament man.

It must in some degree be psychological since the mention of the word can start a player shanking, or should an opponent have a bout of the shanks it can put a doubt in his own mind.

Many pros when asked by a member for a lesson to cure shanking will refuse. They reckon the disease to be more catching than the plague.

And when playing in tournaments it is an unwritten law that the word is never mentioned. If you want to play a shabby trick on an opponent in match play then bring up the subject. Be warned the reply may well be a clip on the chin.

A shank occurs when the ball is struck with the heel of the club instead of the middle of the face.

I'm lucky because the word "shank" never puts any fear into my mind—nor do I mind helping any fellow-pro or amateur if he is a sufferer.

The explanation for such peace of mind is that I can shank a ball on purpose and I reason that if you can do this, knowing what causes the shot, then you must know how to cure it.

One Open champion comes to mind—for obvious reasons I won't give his name—whom I have seen completely circle the green by shanking and finishing almost at the same spot as he started after seven shanks!

I would never ridicule anyone for shanking. Rather it's a question of condolences.

Now for the reason why we shank. There are two that have been well written about, and I offer a third which I think I am the first to set down in print.

What are the two recognised reasons?

The first is a very exaggerated flat inside-to-out swing with perhaps a terrific wrist roll at impact. The ball slides along the face half-way between the centre and the heel and shoots out sideways to the right.

It is unfortunate that this type of shanking can breed more. As the player tries to stop the ball from flying to the right he rolls the clubhead even more and the flatter he swings inside-to-out, rolling the wrists, the more shanks he will produce.

Here's an X-ray of a magnificent shank—with golf writer and handicap four golfer Ben Wright the reluctant victim (PLATE 46).

The second shank is still more common and is produced by swinging far too much inside-to-out with a very stiff-wristed action, that is pushing through the ball and in doing so pushing the club heel straight into it.

Anxiety creeps in here and the more this man shanks the stiffer his swing becomes. So he keeps on pushing his club shank into the ball.

I think we can link this form of shank with the player who has seen frozen photographs of players half-way on the downswing with their wrists fully cocked.

He tries to emulate the position but the clubhead never catches up and his hands are too far ahead of the club face at impact. Which produces a push type of shot, bringing about the shank.

Shanking seems to have increased since the wedge made its introduction in Britain just after World War II, and I think the high-speed camera has also increased the number of sufferers.

With regard to the third form of shank, the one which I have uncovered, I was having some pictures taken by Frank Sowerby and trying deliberately

PLATE 46   Ben Wright and his shank. You can see the inside out path of the clubhead together with a very pronounced rolling of the club at impact. See also the steep line of the hands through the shot.

to shank from certain required positions.

Quite a number of golfers were watching and later that night I heard one man say at the bar "Poor old Ken. He was out there today having his picture taken and he couldn't stop shanking."

What I was actually trying to prove was the part that centrifugal force out of control can play in the shot. I explain more fully later about centrifugal force.

Now for the cures. Go to the practice ground.

Check your grip and see that the inverted "V"'s appear to you, on a bird's-eye view, to go up the middle of the shaft.

Stand comfortably to the ball and do not fall into the trap of thinking you should stand further away as this will only flatten your swing. So stand a normal distance for the club in hand.

While addressing the ball make sure the blade is square to the line of flight and keep it square throughout your backswing.

As an over-correction *feel* you are swinging the club on an outside line while keeping the club low to the ground both going back and through. At the same time *feel* that the clubhead is if anything going across the line of flight (it is almost impossible to shank cutting across the ball).

At no time must there be any tension. The more you play a shot without shanking, the greater will be your relaxed confidence.

It's helpful to feel that the clubhead is going to beat your hands to the ball. Again, this is an over-correction. Start with short pitch shots and work up to a 7-iron trying this method.

You may also like to try holding the club a little further down the grip.

If your mind is pre-occupied with the shank it will possibly help, especially with the really good player, to think of hitting the ball with the toe of the club.

One thing more and then we'll leave the whole subject. The cure for the third type of shank is to have the hands low at address and feel that both wrists are "crooked down" (or low) at the strike.

THE SMOTHER. This is a relative of the hook and when played the ball will fly very low, usually turning to the left. It just won't rise.

The cause is a hooded face at impact. A hooded face being even more pronounced than a closed or shut face.

The smother doesn't happen all that frequently and there is no doubt about the cure. Look to your grip.

The right hand is in too powerful a position under the shaft, which causes the clubhead to turn over at impact.

You may well get away with a 6, 7, 8 or 9-iron because of their loft but once you use less-lofted irons the ball won't get into the air. That's due to the loft being so much reduced.

A player who does this can knock a 6-iron as far as the ordinary player will hit a 3-iron.

The answer to smothering is to make certain your right hand is on top of the shaft with, from a bird's-eye view, the inverted "V"s pointing up the shaft.

CHAPTER FOURTEEN

One Continuous Swing

This is a chapter I have been waiting to write. So far I have been out-lining stage by stage the basic teachings of golf.

Such groundwork has its value but at some points I passed it on with reluctance—as I will now explain.

You may recall how in chapter four I mentioned that I hated breaking down the swing into its five separate movements. There is no other way to give that necessary information.

But reducing the swing to small pieces offends me deeply as a teaching professional. By doing so I almost feel false to myself and develop a guilt complex.

What I have done is pull apart what should be a smooth movement to explain what happens. And what I set down is in some ways misguided and untrue!

To make amends let me pass on my whole golf philosophy, teaching and experience in one short paragraph:

THE SWING IS ONE CONTINUOUS UNBROKEN MOVEMENT FROM START TO FINISH AND ALL YOU NEED TO THINK ABOUT IS THE PATH YOU WISH THE CLUBHEAD TO TAKE.

Read that again because in those words you have the secret of good golf. I promised to make the game as simple as possible and strip it of so many unnecessary complications and mystiques.

There really is no need to make this a hard game. Many golfers play badly not because they are incapable of good golf but because they are thinking wrongly.

If you concentrate on thinking of the path that you want the clubhead to follow then you can clear your head of any thought involving the movements of shoulder, hip, knee, foot, etc., etc., that take place.

Or as the late Ernest Jones, to my mind the greatest teacher in the history of golf, once explained: "You don't make movement to move the clubhead, you move the clubhead to make movement."

Exactly.

Just to get this important lesson 100 per cent clear I am saying that those professionals or instruction books that concentrate on the hundred-and-one movements, large and small, involved in a golf swing, and then ask you to put the various pieces together, have their priorities wrong.

They are putting the cart before the horse and making life complicated for the pupil.

I would go so far as to say that many famous world-beaters, where their movements are concerned, are not aware what they are doing.

You have no need to worry about knee, shoulder and the rest. Just concentrate on producing a free and uninterrupted swing along the desired path.

Do that and all the other actions will happen anyway. Now that's rock-bottom simplicity, isn't it?

The way to master golf is a combination of rhythmic swing, with active hands, and the natural response to your thought about the line you wish the clubhead to follow.

Let me give an illustration about how the body responds to clubhead movement.

A player comes to see me and says he has been making some mistakes on the course and his partner thinks the fault is that he has been turning his right shoulder into the shot.

My reply is that there is no doubt your friend means well and is trying to help. In what he has *seen* he is perfectly correct. You are throwing your right shoulder into the shot.

But for every effect there has to be a cause. I could ask the player not to turn his shoulder into the shot, instead I would rather he hit some balls with his present swing.

What I want to learn is what makes his shoulder turn into the shot. Once I've done that I can give him a remedial thought—likely as not involving the clubhead path—which will stop him turning his shoulder into the ball.

That is response to clubhead movement.

I believe a lot of amateurs would be far better players if they thought less about the individual movements they are making.

It was a point I made in discussions with a friend who is a dentist and a top-class amateur. I told him that in order to bring together the drill (that's the club) and the tooth (the ball) he had to make various movements.

He probably had no idea exactly what those movements were but if he tried to put together the same movements consciously, in order to end with the drill and tooth in contact, he would very likely make a hash of it.

In advancing my theory of concentrating on the desired clubhead path you will appreciate that I am not giving you something you can see, something tangible.

I know that confuses some pupils. So many players when they have a lesson want to be given advice involving something they can see—get that knee in quicker, move your hand over, don't pivot so far, try this grip. And so on.

Tell them to think about the correct clubhead path and they feel cheated somehow.

I've mentioned the fact that a clock pendulum swings to-and-fro in constant perpendicular movement. As golfers we are seeking something similar.

But since we have to bend over the ball throughout the swing the clubhead path has to follow an inclined plane. Then, of course, we are adding a strike within that swing.

Any movement we make is a response to a thought and the parts of the body involved will act accordingly. Take a simple action such as a small boy throwing a stone.

He has two things in mind—the stone itself, and propelling it towards the target.

Just consider the instinctive movements required to carry out the action. There will be transfer of weight from one foot to the other, arms stretched out, muscles flexed . . . you could get a whole chapter out of what happens.

Try to make all these movements in sequence and a very jerky action would result.

As we get older we should all grow wiser. When I first set off on the tournament trail I would change my swing regularly, trying to copy the action of the golfer of the day.

I know now that this you just cannot do. *Once you have learned the basics and brought to them your own personal characteristics that is the swing you have to cultivate and learn to live with.*

Had I appreciated that truism 20 years ago then I would have done better in competition. But there is compensation in that I can pass on what I learned by my own mistakes.

It was Jimmy Adams, the well-known Ryder Cup Scot, who quoted to me Ernest Jones' words about moving the clubhead to make movement.

This took a little while to sink in but I realised that unknowingly I had been teaching that advice for a long, long time. I had always told my pupils to swing the clubhead in the correct arc and argued that the body movements would be responsive.

Much as with the small boy throwing that stone.

When the clubhead is swung back the right side turns out of the way to allow a free passage to the clubhead going back. The instruction books call this the pivot.

You are bending over at address, so it is only natural that your left shoulder comes under your chin.

You are now set to deliver the blow and instinctively you swing the clubhead back to the ball. To provide a free passage your left side turns out of the way and the swing is complete.

One continuous movement and not a succession of small individual movements. Right?

Next we have to swing the golf club with something and the only part of the body in contact with the club is the hands.

So it follows that your hands are the most sensitive part of your body in the golf swing. Whatever you want the golf ball to do your hands alone will respond to that thought.

And whatever your hands do in conjunction with the clubhead, then the body will respond to that thought.

I find far too much confusion these days in golf teaching, with club golfers becoming increasingly confused by books and articles by well-known players.

Some of these "names" are still at a tender age and I fear that they write their books by having their own pictures taken, studying them, and writing about what they see.

This doesn't help the reader because he tries to put together frozen movements—which makes it impossible to hit a golf ball with an unbroken swing.

You must not analyse a golf swing in this way because you become too conscious of the frozen positions.

You start thinking of what positions the various parts of the body should be in, and that means that the all-important clubhead and hands become secondary.

You'll never hit a golf ball properly while thinking about half-a-dozen different points.

We've all knocked a nail into a piece of wood. It doesn't need a second thought. But you could make it difficult by thinking about the movements involved.

Children are great mimics and if you have a child keen to get into the game then take him or her to watch some good players when they are competing locally.

A child doesn't look at all the complicated movements taking place but assimilates instead the overall picture of the swing.

Hand the child a small club and more often than not he will repeat exactly what he has seen. My own 13-year-old son, Kelvin, is a good example.

PLATE 46A   My son Kelvin, 13, has produced this swing purely by concentrating on clubhead path. With this type of photograph the ball is still seen on the page although it has in fact been struck.

Look at this picture of him (PLATE 46A). He has learned to swing like this mainly by watching first-class players at tournaments.

I have given him a little instruction but NEVER involving individual movements. All I do, when he has gone wrong, is show him in what direction the clubhead should be swung.

Knowing, of course, that by telling him the path the clubhead should follow, the correct body movements would follow that direction.

He had a habit of picking the club up too sharply from the ground.

This naturally caused his wrists to break very sharply—the responsive action to picking the club up.

I didn't tell him to swing back not breaking his wrists so soon. Rather I said to keep the clubhead low to the ground as long as possible.

Which has the desired effect of keeping the wrist break until later in the swing.

By teaching that way I am keeping his mind on the clubhead—which is where we want the power—and not on his wrists.

Whatever part you are thinking of is where you put the power. If you wish to be a consistent golfer then the clubhead must never be secondary.

Picking the clubhead up too sharply is a common fault caused by the feeling that the ball has got to be hammered down. This movement is very wrong. The proper way to hit a golf ball is to strike it forward, leaving the loft of the club to take it into the air. This means the clubhead must be swung back low along the ground, and, in keeping low brushing the grass, your arms will automatically stay quite straight. You will have a wide arc on the backswing and the correct position at the top, which in turn will help provide greater power and accuracy at impact.

I come now to my X-ray photos, which prove without doubt that the arc in which you swing the clubhead—in one smooth movement—is all important.

Incidentally, Ernest Jones regretted we could not see our own swing when hitting a shot. We can today through Frank Sowerby's X-ray swing photos.

All right, argue that we still cannot see it . . . but we can see the path.

When I first had my X-ray pictures taken I was quite pleased with the result (see PLATE 1, page   ) until I saw those of others.

I could see that I was different from the top of my backswing where my lines ran parallel for a while. Yet in most of the other players' pictures the lines parted immediately from the end of the top of the backswing to the beginning of the downswing.

Without making any conscious body movement but by thinking of the clubhead only and the path I wanted it to take you can see the difference when I had a second X-ray session (PLATE 47).

I am also hitting the ball a greater distance and with more consistency. So one is always learning—although the improvement would not have been possible without the X-ray analysis.

I want to end this chapter by quoting Ernest Jones once more:

"The trouble is that the various members of the body including the shoulders were normally anxious to get busy too strenuously and too soon, and that the only way of insuring their working in due co-ordination with the other members of the body, notably the hands and fingers, was to treat them not as disastrous leaders, but as wholly admirable followers."

The heavy body muscles nearly always want to move first or too soon when we are hitting hard.

Remember that these muscles are only useful in supplying power. Swing the clubhead and let the hands deliver that power.

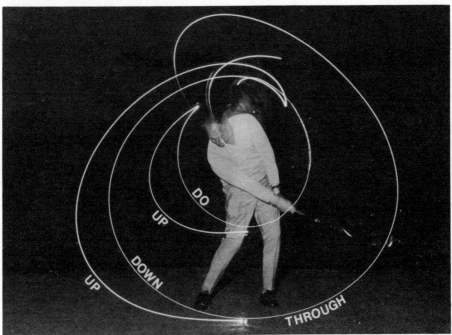

PLATE 47   Compare this picture with the first X-ray I had taken— (Plate 1). It looks and is a much better action, particularly in regard to the width between the upswing and downswing. So I too have learned something from the X-ray pictures.

CHAPTER FIFTEEN

X-ray Analysis

Now to outline how these unique X-ray pictures of golf stars in action can be read and analysed—and also explaining how they can help club golfers to learn more of what is happening during a swing.

To my mind, and in this I have the support of various authorities, these X-rays really extend our knowledge of a great game. They prove some long-held theories to be right, and disprove others.

In summary they show:

Contrary to accepted opinion the downswing is not only *outside* the backswing, but the difference is very pronounced;

Our best tournament players all appear to swing from slightly out-to-in;

The swing path of the driver is more oval than circular, although the path grows more circular as you move through the clubs until reaching the wedge, by which time it is quite round;

As the clubhead speeds up the line gets thinner, this being most noticeable around the impact area;

Weight transfer occurs after impact and not before;

The wider the swing and the farther apart the up and down lines on the backswing, the greater the power;

Where lines run parallel at the top of the backswing (as with Dai Rees and myself) the man is an open-to-shut player, whereas when the lines part straight away at the top of the backswing (Neil Coles, Billy Casper and others) they belong to a closed-to-open player.

They also convince me that a partly shut-faced player has less trouble getting the clubhead through square at impact than an open-to-shut player who opens the face on the backswing and fights to get it square again for the strike. There is less room for error with a partly shut-faced player.

These X-rays are positive proof of how the clubhead behaves and the actual path it takes.

PLATE 48 Superb action shots of Neil Coles showing positively that the path of the backswing is outside that of the downswing. Doesn't it look a marvellous action!

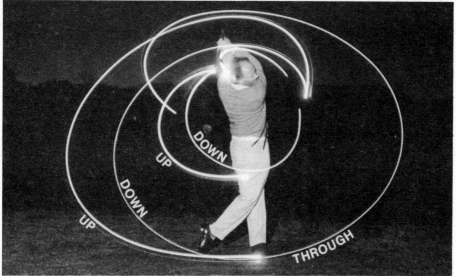

My first surprise on studying the evidence was that the clubhead arc was much more oval than I had imagined. Neil Coles had the same reaction. You can see his swing in detail here (PLATE 48). Frank Sowerby took

PLATE 49   Here are two outstanding old and new world swings X-rayed. Both Tony Jacklin and Billy Casper are seen from in front and also looking down the line of flight. Once again the line of the downswing is outside that of the backswing.

I

about thirty pictures of him driving and the thing which astonished Neil was that his swing was so repetitive.

It's almost possible to place all his negatives on top of each other and see only one swing—which proves how grooved his swing has become.

All the X-rays of world beaters and top stars like Casper, Huggett, Rees, Dave Thomas, Peter Alliss, Jimmy Adams, Bernard Hunt and Tony Jacklin show without exception that they do *not* appear to swing from inside-to-out (PLATE 49) *see page 128 and 129.*

Yet the theory has always been that the correct swing is from in-to-out.

Again, without exception, with all these players the path of the downswing is outside the path of the backswing—yet every golf book has told us that the correct way to swing is with the downswing inside that of the backswing.

This apparent slightly out-to-in swing among the "greats" was my biggest surprise, although I had thought it possible for some time after watching them play and noting that their divots were always across the line of flight.

If you are left with any doubts then try to look at the bottom of any outstanding player's driver. You will find that the line of past shots runs from heel to toe across the sole plate.

If they were swinging from in-to-out as we have all been taught then those lines would run the other way. Scientific analysis declares that among the "greats" the clubhead travels straight for a while at impact. But the X-ray pictures prove conclusively this DOES NOT happen.

Perhaps I had better explain next why earlier I asked you not to copy the stars' slightly out-to-in swing but asked you to work instead on an in-to-out swing.

The natural way to swing as we know is from out-to-in. With a small degree of exaggeration this produces a slice or a pull.

To minimise or combat this effect I teach an over-correction by telling the pupil to feel he is swinging from in-to-out and attacking the ball from the inside.

What you get then is a state of neutrality between the natural and the taught swing which mostly produces a straight ball.

I'm not saying that you cannot swing from inside-to-out. You can—but these under pressure are the hookers and pushers.

My advice to club golfers is to *feel* you are swinging inside-to-out yet knowing all the while that nature is making the clubhead path less in-to-out than you imagine.

The star tournament player has practised the "unnatural" in-to-out swing for so long that it has become natural for him. He also no doubt feels he is swinging slightly inside-to-out but, as the X-rays show, that is not so.

You should be able to feel you are swinging along the same path as the top professionals are displaying in the X-rays taken from the front.

Do *not* try to copy the action as these same players have been caught from behind looking down the line of flight.

Copy the front shots and you will then be thinking of the clubhead path, which is what I want.

I discussed the surprising slightly out-to-in swing evidence with Neil Coles. He told me that whenever he is hitting the ball badly his divots are either pointing to the right or straight.

But when he is hitting the ball well then his divots are across the line of flight from outside-to-in.

I will admit however that poorer players hit the ball more outside-to-in than the stars. By the way, a player who hits across the ball, out-to-in, will possibly never shank.

Checking the X-rays you can see that the hands move in much more of a circle than the clubhead and the white line of the hands disappears during the follow-through.

The reason is that the right thumb light turns away from the camera during the "black out" and reappears near the end of the follow-through.

This "black out" is caused by the rolling of the hands, after impact.

In the X-rays of both Coles and myself the clubhead has gone very wide through the ball on the follow-through, with the result that the clubhead will stay with the ball for quite a while. Which helps distance and accuracy.

On the pictures taken from behind the line of flight it is noticeable that the line made by the clubhead disappears shortly after the clubhead starts the downward path. It reappears on entering the hitting area.

This tells us that as the clubhead comes back to the ball it is being held back in the cocked position although the arms are moving down—which is why the light is hidden from the camera.

The light reappears as the clubhead squares up just before impact as it catches up with the hands.

You can also see that the line of the hands at impact is above the starting position. This is due to centrifugal force. The hands arch at impact, denoting force in this area.

I have other X-rays with the head in four different positions: at address, after moving slightly back at impact, forward towards the end of the follow-through, and over left foot at completion of swing.

Which proves that weight transfer comes *after* impact and not before.

It also illustrates the presence of opposing movements, with the clubhead going forward and the body momentarily going in the other direction.

The pictures in general—line of the clubhead on the way down being inside the line of the clubhead on the backswing—prove that the wider path of the backswing and the narrowed path of the downswing produce more power, coupled with accuracy.

This is why a small man can sometimes outdrive a bigger man when both have similar capabilities.

When I showed Dai Rees the X-rays he said "This is fantastic. I've never seen anything like this done before."

He noted the break in the hand-line of Neil Coles' follow-through and remarked: "If Neil could swing so that the line is continuous throughout the follow-through then this would give him the action which would make him the world's finest golfer, driving through the ball further before allowing the hands to turn over."

I do not agree with him on this point as I believe the hands should turn over a little—late after impact. This means that at some time during the follow-through the hand light will disappear from the camera for a fraction of a second.

What would be wrong, though, is for the light to vanish almost immediately after impact.

This would indicate the face of the club being closed too soon and not keeping square to the line of flight long enough.

I was able to help that capable Ryder Cup performer, George Will, through an X-ray session. His pictures showed he was too narrow in his follow-through and was hitting a shade too late.

Obviously I was not giving such a noted student of the game a lesson, but George was pleased to see as fact what he had thought himself might be his faults.

He told me after practising for one week that he was flighting the ball better than for months and was hitting it 20 yards farther.

I finish with some food for thought for those critics who say that good players swing from inside-to-out. At the Augusta National course where the American Masters is played a picture taken at the 180 yards par three 12th hole shows that 95 per cent of the divot marks were across the line of flight from out-to-in.

CHAPTER SIXTEEN

Some New Theories

We have all read in instruction books that during the movement from the top of the backswing back to the ball the weight must be transferred to the left foot.

This is NOT so.

I will agree, however, that the left foot does go flat on the ground as the downswing commences. It is an optical illusion that the weight has been transferred before the ball has been struck—or even immediately after.

When striking the ball all good players, who are invariably long hitters, have their weight behind the ball. Or, put another way, their centre of gravity.

Here is a shot we have taken of Dave Thomas, who is one of the longest and straightest hitters in the world. (PLATE 50) *see page 134.* You can see that two-thirds of his weight is plainly behind the ball well after impact.

You cannot have it both ways. It is impossible to have your weight on your left foot and keep the centre of gravity behind the ball at the same time.

I will take it still further and say that as you enter the hitting area, with the clubhead going through the ball and towards the target, so the player's head moves BACK in the opposite direction.

Sometimes as much as six inches from the place it occupied at address.

This is opposing movement—clubhead going one way and head the other. It happens momentarily and is much more pronounced in first-class players.

For a simple example that your weight MUST be behind the ball when it is struck, consider a boxer delivering a blow. The whole weight of his body is behind his fist (PLATE 51) *see page 135.*

There would be no force behind the blow if he were alongside his opponent. That would mean his body would be in front of his hands.

PLATE 50   Long hitter Dave Thomas. The flash has caught him with
his weight still well behind the ball.

The X-ray photographs prove what I am saying is a fact. It may look
as if the weight is on the left foot at impact but a line drawn through the
body and downwards to the ball shows that the centre of gravity is behind
this line.

It also means that the centre of gravity is behind the ball and the head
has moved in the opposite direction to the clubhead.

What I do concede, though, is that as the swing nears completion THEN
the weight has transferred to the left.

Now for a warning: do NOT try to make this movement consciously. It
will happen if you allow the clubhead to start to pass your hands and body
at the moment of impact. It will happen naturally if you swing correctly
with the hands.

Should you encounter any difficulty keeping behind the ball what you
can do is imagine that your left cheek is at the back of the ball as the clubhead begins to pass the hands at impact. That will produce the desired
opposing movement.

But if your head moves to the left with the clubhead at the moment of
strike (the cause of hitting too late) then power and direction will be lost.

There hasn't been much written about opposing movement.

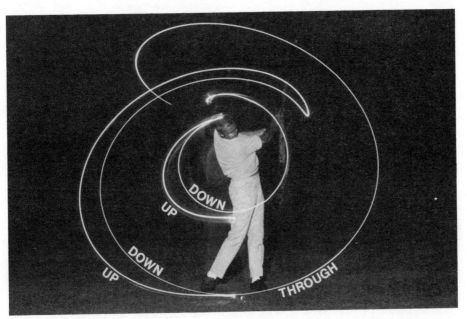

PLATE 51   Drive the 007 way. This is screen star Sean Connery showing the swing that beat Goldfinger. Once again the weight is back behind the ball even though his swing has almost finished. A commendable action.

Isaac Newton knew about it—even if he wasn't a golfer. Newton's Law is that for every force there must be an equal and opposing force.

The result of this Law in golf being that the two countering forces keep your swing well balanced and repeating.

But these opposing movements, I repeat, are not consciously manufactured. Take a look at the best players getting ready to strike. Their first movement, to get the feel of the forthcoming shot, is what is commonly called the "waggle".

You will notice that as he moves the clubhead right in the waggle his knees move in the other direction. That is, to the left.

It happens subconsciously and is nature's way of creating perfect balance.

Another example is the forward press which happens immediately prior to the clubhead being swung at the start of the backswing.

I am frequently being asked by pupils "Would it help if I had a forward press like So-and-So?"

My answer is always that whether we want one or not we all have a forward press on beginning a backswing and there is no need for any conscious effort.

Once again this is opposing movement, with the hands moving very slightly to the left as the clubhead goes in the opposite direction.

For an athletic version of our forward press think of a runner preparing to leave his starting block. What does he do? He pushes back with one foot to make his body go forward.

Which brings me to another subject rarely mentioned in golf books: centrifugal force.

I am positive today that centrifugal force out of control is a vital factor in shanking.

During any swing centrifugal force is at its greatest power when the clubhead has reached maximum speed. The only thing to keep this power harnessed, preventing it from getting out of control, is that part of the body which holds the club—your hands.

The X-rays provide the proof that when a ball is struck at full power centrifugal force makes both wrists "stretch" at impact. They could even arch.

One result of this wrist action, which is responsive, is that the clubhead pushes forward and out.

The whole body stretches up, so much so in some cases that in some pictures of top-class players they are almost on their toes at impact.

It is most essential in golf that you have strong hands to stop this force from getting out of control . . . should it get out of control it could cause shanking.

The only way to produce centrifugal force is to swing the club. If you use a jerky motion instead then there is no such force.

Centrifugal force helps to give power to the shot and stems from the centre of the swing.

We have the example of the hammer thrower and the shot putter, both of whom are throwing an object weighing the same amount.

The shot putter can only achieve a relatively short distance but the hammer man, who is bringing centrifugal force into play, can swing it and send it, thanks to centrifugal force, many times farther.

For an example of centrifugal force out of control take a dynamo. It spins and exerts outward force which is centrifugal force.

If that outward force were stronger than the casing harnessing it then the whole machine would fly to pieces.

The lesson is that you can only strike a ball as hard as your hands will allow . . . so strengthen them to achieve greater harnessed power.

CHAPTER SEVENTEEN

You Need Hands

The hands are the tools of the brain—and of paramount importance in the golf swing.

Only the hands are in contact with the club. Only the hands can control the clubhead. And just as a chain is only as strong as its weakest link, so a player is only as good as his hands.

They are an essential part of your body and used continually during everyday life. You use them almost subconsciously.

When you use your hands other parts of the body respond instinctively. You don't have to think. So naturally it must be that your hands are leaders.

You cannot play good golf unless you have good hands. They hold, swing and guide the club and it is through them that you feel the movement you wish to pass on to the clubhead. Through feel they respond to a thought . . . which in golf is the direction you wish the clubhead to travel.

But remember the body acts in response to the intention and movement of the hands. Don't let the hands become secondary, reacting to body movements.

You have to learn to swing the clubhead before you can play well.

As I explained previously it is possible to develop a low-handicap player's movements, possibly through practising body movements, but if you have not developed a swing through using your hands you can still have a 24-handicap hand action.

Although the hands are leaders responding to a thought, I am not asking you to have your mind centred on your hands when swinging the club.

Your mind ought to be fixed on the clubhead and the path on which you have been taught to swing it—coupled with this, of course, is the golf ball and the strike within the swing.

As the hands start to swing the clubhead back to the ball the body responds by turning, very much like the hub of a wheel.

What you can do is try to make your hands stronger in relation to your body. Should you be a strong individual but weak in your hands then they will act as a resistant (as in an electric circuit) and will be unable to deliver the power created by your body. This is the reason why a slightly built player with strong hands can outdrive a seemingly powerful player.

The clubhead must be travelling at its greatest speed just after impact. It results in the ball staying in contact longer with the clubhead—the secret of long hitting.

What it means is that the clubhead is still catching the ball up. You get the feel of the ball squeezing itself into the clubhead—a soft feel. When the opposite happens, that is clubhead losing speed, you feel a hard jarring.

All of us are built differently. Some with quick reflexes, others with slow.

You cannot build up any greater speed than your physical ability allows you to swing the clubhead.

If you are a relatively short hitter yet your movements are correct then you lack clubhead speed and I am afraid you will have to live with it.

You will not create greater speed by throwing your heavy body muscles into the shot—which is heaving.

Mathematically Energy is $\dfrac{Mass \times Velocity^2}{2}$

Which in golfing terms becomes

$$\frac{Clubhead\ Weight \times Speed^2}{2}$$

Don't look at this equation, however, and run immediately for the heaviest club you can find. If it is too heavy and you are not strong enough to swing it you will lack all the essential clubhead speed.

However, assuming that you are swinging the clubhead correctly yet lack the ability to create speed in the striking area, then nine times out of ten it must be that your hands are weak and are not delivering the power your body is supplying.

What I would suggest as a remedy is to build up the strength of the hands with various exercises, the best method being to knead a rubber ball that will fit into the palm of your hand. Or there are various spring devices which are readily available on the market.

If you work on this diligently you will be surprised with the result.

The left hand is the guiding hand, while the right produces the strike and makes the clubhead catch up with the hands at impact. I much prefer to think of them, though, working in unison.

Ideally at impact you should be in a similar position as you were at address with arms straight, so maintaining the wide radius of your swing.

CHAPTER EIGHTEEN

The Late Hit

More than 85 per cent of the club golfers I teach and watch all have the same fault—a slice. And in the majority of cases it is caused by a hit which is too late.

They delay the uncocking of the wrists so long that the clubface does not have time to square itself before contact is made with the ball.

What I do with pupils who are suffering in this way is give them an over-correction, telling them that the only thought in their mind from the top of the backswing should be to get the clubhead to the ball first.

The clubhead must begin to pass the hands at the moment of impact, but many of them are leaving it behind. By thinking of getting the clubhead to the ball first they will automatically release their wrist cock earlier.

One of the biggest villains in the game today is the high-speed camera.

It's a very desirable modern invention—but it "lies". The result being golfing miseries and mis-interpretations.

What would you say is the most photographed action in golf today?

For my money, and as I have to iron out pupils' faults that's exactly what it does bring me, it's the picture of the tournament pro with his hands waist high on the downswing, wrists cocked, about to "hit late" (PLATE 52) *see page 140*.

Sorry, camera, but there's no such thing as late hitting in the first-class player. You see, what the high-speed camera doesn't show is that the clubhead, at the late-hitting position, is catching up the hands all the time.

So that by the time the ball is reached both hands and clubhead are together. As usual there is an exception to this late-hitting theory. That's the push wedge shot and a special case.

But if we're thinking about the majority of golf shots, then late hitting is a myth.

Yet all the books and magazines make regular reference to pictures of

PLATE 52   This is typical of the Late Hit Position pictures seen so often. Don't copy this position but do understand the powers that produce it.

late hitting. My teaching has always been that the way to good golf is to get the clubhead to the ball first—or feel you are.

The opposite to late is early. I don't like to use that because if you ask a golfer to hit "early" he is likely to start hitting from the top.

I much prefer to use the word "sooner" to a player who has got into the habit of hitting too late.

In the days before lightning photography we used to see the same "late hitting" pictures, except that the photograph contained a blur made up of shaft and clubhead.

From this it could be seen that the clubhead was catching up the hands. But that vital factor is missing from the high-speed photo.

I get any number of pupils coming to me and adopting their "late hitting" position. "I believe this is right," they say. "The photos show that I have to get the clubhead and wrists like this. Only now you're telling me to get the clubhead to the ball first."

When they try out the advice I usually hear "Well, how do you account for that? I'm hitting the ball much farther."

Let's break it down. The backswing is for one thing only and that is to take the clubhead back to the top in order to gather enough speed to hit the ball an appreciable distance.

It's exactly the same when you swing an axe to chop down a tree. It's the distance you take the axe back that gives time to gather speed and power on the way down for the moment of impact.

The high-speed camera catches the player two-thirds of the way down to the ball with wrists fully cocked. It looks as if he has purposely reached this position in order to hit late.

So the handicap man reasons that what is good enough for the stars must be good enough for him. But when he tries to copy the pictures he can only do so by "freezing" the movement.

Agreed, his wrists are cocked. But it's still a frozen movement.

This produces a locked position as it were, and there is no time now to release the clubhead with any force. Invariably he will hit the ball only at the speed of his shoulder turn.

The wrist-cocking action takes place anyway without him consciously trying to achieve it.

What it really means when he tries to ape the picture position is that he might just as well have swung back only as far as that point.

Wrist-cocking takes place automatically because when the clubhead is swung to the top of the backswing your wrists do not cock fully until they are *on the way back* to the ball, so producing a subconscious type of flail.

The reason for this is involved with a change of direction: from the clubhead going up to starting the clubhead down, the force is so great that the wrists, so long as you are relaxed, will break more fully on the way down than they do on the way up.

Furthermore, there is no such thing as the clubhead reaching the top of the backswing. Why? Because the clubhead is *still going back* when you are in fact returning to the ball.

On the backswing you get to about shoulder high with the hands. From that point you will start returning the clubhead to the ball.

What happens is that the "changing direction" force, plus the weight of the club, keeps the clubhead going up while you are beginning to come down.

Consider the example of an aircraft in a dive. As the plane pulls out of the dive it is still for a moment going down. Much the same takes place in the golf swing.

While you're going back to the ball the clubhead is still rising. And, of course, this natural full-wrist break happens.

It will not happen, though, if the player is gripping too tight or is too tense. These two faults produce that "frozen" movement.

When the handicap player tries to reproduce the pro position and hit late he is almost certain to hit too late himself.

The hands have not allowed the clubhead to pass at the second of impact; they have gone past the ball before the clubhead has arrived. Which is striking too late.

What the high-speed picture cannot show is that after the tournament player has been "frozen", his clubhead will move through almost half a circle while the hands will possibly move only about one foot from the right to left thigh.

Go back to the aircraft example. When a plane banks the outer wing travels farther and must travel faster than the inner wing. The outer wing is our clubhead and the inner wing our hands.

In order to help the ordinary player who has become a victim of late hitting I pass on what I know to be an over-correction.

I tell him to feel that once the clubhead is returning from the "mythical" top of the backswing it will arrive at the ball first.

What actually happens is that clubhead and hands arrive at the same time.

There's another example in a line of soldiers ordered to wheel. The out-side man has more ground to cover and has to be much quicker than the inside man.

In the same way the clubhead must move faster than the hands.

I find it will help any player to know subconsciously all the time where the clubhead is, and remembering that although it has farther to travel it must get to the ball at the same time, approximately, as the hands.

The high-speed camera is probably responsible for starting more golfers off on the wrong path than almost any other factor.

The man who copies the position lacks distance with his shots because he has no clubhead speed at impact. When you hit too late you achieve maximum clubhead speed a long while after the ball has been struck.

Many club golfers slice as a result and then try to hit later seeking a cure. This only enlarges the fault.

If you want to see the full story of what the top men are up to when they reach that "frozen" waistland sort out some real old-time pictures. That blur gives the answer.

To finish, a few more thoughts about the backswing. If you have trouble keeping your left arm comfortably straight then let it bend a little. Make sure, though, that it is straight at impact.

The backswing is the most important part of the swing. As you swing the clubhead should start by going round in a semi-circle. Never consciously make the clubhead go straight back along the intended line of flight otherwise your club is trying to go straight while your body is rotating. You will no doubt sway back with the clubhead.

Start the backswing thinking in terms of smoothness and try not to break your wrists too soon.

CHAPTER NINETEEN

It's all in the Mind

So far I have dealt mainly with the physical side of golf. But I would like to point out now how important it is to be strong mentally.

Particularly, of course, when a player is under pressure. One of the most-heard comments about golf from experienced players is "It's all in the mind."

I have had the opportunity of discussing the mental side of golf with a psychiatrist, who is also a low single-figure golfer, and another medical man.

I told them that in my own experience it was likely that a player who was weaker physically but stronger mentally would beat an opponent who was better physically but not so strong in his mental approach.

Both players, one assumes, hit the ball excellently when not under pressure. Naturally, in most cases, the physically stronger would hit the ball farther.

But the moment pressure comes into the game I would back the other man every time. In golf it isn't true that a good big 'un will always beat a good little 'un.

And with my size I should know!

When I write of being "strong mentally" what I wish to put over is that if you can dismiss everything from your mind except the shot about to be played, then pressure is not likely to ruin it.

I think it is essential to learn to form a mental picture of the shot about to be played. It takes training and practice, but that mind picture will set your body up automatically for the stroke to come.

In the case of the player who is weak in mental approach, while he may have a picture of the shot about to be played he does NOT wholly keep out the fear of what might happen should the shot go wrong.

This mental picture of possible disaster dominates his concentration.

For a single example take the matter of playing a new course. The like-

lihood is that you will play it very well. This is because you lack any knowledge of the hidden dangers.

Not a worry about out-of-bounds, ditches, bunkers, and the rest. Except
that on the way round you make a mental note of the trouble that might
have been met.

So that by the second or third round you become conscious that disaster
may be lurking at certain holes. And if the mental picture of the trouble
spots is greater than concentration on the ideal shot to be played then
invariably you hit the ball to the area which has been nagging you.

But think positively and the desired shot will materialise . . . in which
case the good big 'un would always beat the good little 'un.

I have noticed in matches the reaction to a casual remark such as "The
out of bounds is very close on this hole, isn't it?"

The man addressed, if not strong mentally, is left with a dominant picture
of the trouble spot mentioned and will swing the clubhead in that direction.

It goes to show just how important to your overall game are the mental
images that you form.

When it comes to failure under pressure I would say that 85 per cent of
golf is mental and only 15 per cent is physical ability. The reason I give
such a high percentage to mental approach is that under pressure mental
approach will always dominate physical application and movement.

There are various forms of mental interference. Take the player who
dwells on different parts of his swing while on the course. Whatever part he
thinks about while swinging the clubhead, that's where the centre of power
will be found.

It's worth emphasising once again that when playing in a match all you
should be thinking of is swinging the clubhead on the desired path, and of
making contact with the ball. That, with a picture of the coming shot, is
enough.

Most of us know what happens when we strike a ball but few appreciate
what is going on inside our mind.

I have studied the mental side of the game and try to teach mentally.

Each player is an individual and I like to find out how he is thinking
before tackling his golf problems. The basics never alter, but I vary the
way of imparting them according to the player's physical and mental
characteristics.

As I have explained, my rock-bottom teaching is that the hands are the
key factor to the whole swing and that your body will respond to what your
hands are doing.

I think of my brain as a computer, and before playing a shot there are

K

many things to be taken into consideration. Shall I explain that?

The movements of the swing are governed by the hands, and they in turn are controlled by the greatest computer of all, the brain.

Our senses are smell, sight, feel, hearing, and taste. But the most important of all, when thinking of golf, is positional sense—or posture.

When setting yourself up for a shot your eyes take in the general terrain and distances involved. Through feel you have the sense of knowing where the clubhead is throughout the swing.

Hearing is important because you might take in distractions. Wind, for instance, can disturb your hearing. Personally, I can never play a shot successfully should a train be passing or an aircraft flying overhead. The reason, I believe, is that like some other players I am sensitive to the swishing sound of a club.

All these things are fed into the brain computer, which not only sets you up for the shot but also determines the result of the stroke.

The experienced player can feed the computer information to produce the required shot. Equally if the wrong information is fed then the resulting answer will be wrong.

I also believe that through playing under different conditions the mind logs various "happenings" which emerge later as experience stored at subconscious level.

When I played regularly in tournaments I could never understand why I played so well in practice but sometimes folded up when the big day arrived. Yet I felt I was as good as the next man.

Some people said it was nervousness. I did at the time. Not any more.

I believe that when pressure is off you play the shot you have in mind with no outside interference. But when under pressure a disastrous picture seems to loom over the positive part, and the wrong picture is stronger than the correct one you want to transmit to your physical side.

Changing under pressure is most common and has happened to many players who are otherwise great strikers of the ball.

So now we have to obliterate the disastrous picture from our mind. But can this part of our mental approach be altered? Can it be minimised? Does constant practice help? Or regular playing in tournaments?

The funny thing is that while I could "see" the mental make-up in first-class players I was unable to see it in myself (PLATE 53).

I have known many young players and predicted who would be mediocre, who would be good, and who would be great.

What, I asked my medical friends, can the "mentally weaker" golfer do to maintain his game under pressure and lessen the effect on his golf?

PLATE 53 I went over for the Canadian Open recently and these two Indians said "How". So I showed them. I hope they're better with tomahawks than they are with a 5-iron! They must have been satisfied— I've still got my hair.

The psychiatrist began by emphasising the importance of concentration and said it could be affected in two ways.

There is external stimulus, easy to understand, caused by cameras clicking, somebody moving, or a match being struck, for instance.

Then there is internal stimulus coming from within the player as anxiety. In an anxious personality the anxiety comes to the surface (moving from the subconscious to the conscious) and interferes with concentration.

A mentally stronger player tends to repress these anxieties into his subconscious. On the other hand, we all know some anxiety. It's a defence mechanism. Yet we don't want too much of a good thing.

When a person is frightened he sweats, shakes and gets into a tremor. His co-ordination vanishes. Anxiety on the course takes effect in different ways.

Say a man is worried about shanking and his fellow players happen to mention shanking. This keeps his anxiety going and perpetuates it at conscious level . . .

But the stronger personality is able to repress his mental fear, so that when someone says "Don't you dare shank" he is able to laugh it off and play his normal shot.

The warning stays in his subconscious as opposed to the other fellow, who brings it to conscious level and feeds his anxiety.

The effects will remain until he can bury his fears and phobias below conscious level. But a few bad shots or some pressure will bring it to the surface.

Take a foolish shot into a bunker. The player sees the bunker, becomes anxious, and as a result that is where the ball goes. Co-ordination and concentration trouble again.

The point being that it's not the bunker causing the trouble. It's fear.

Worth mentioning, too, that once a player is about to enter the hitting area of his stroke no outside distraction will penetrate until after the ball has been struck. The reason being that his concentration at this particular moment is too great.

When it comes to the difference between good and great players there are three factors to consider:

1. Physical make-up. Build is pretty much a fixture and it may or may not be suitable for a certain sport. It is possible to overcome some physical disability and get reasonably good through constant practice.

2. Mental approach.

3. An inherent quality. This is something you cannot acquire. It seems you are born with it. This inherent quality allows a player to make the fullest use of his physical and mental talent.

When a player over a period of time regularly does well in practice but badly in tournaments then his failure is due to anxious personality.

It may be crazy but such a player goes from plus golf in practice to ten handicap in a competition. The blame belongs to pressure and anxiety.

I put some questions to the medical experts and I am sure their answers will help all golfers. Here they are:

Q. Golf is a still ball game, which is more difficult than a moving ball game. Is this due to the fact that a player has too long to think before playing a shot?

A. Yes, that is so. The anxious type of player can take too long to consider and absorb the distractions round him. In a moving ball game reactions are almost at reflex level.

Q. How, then, can he minimise anxiety?

A. By continuous practice and thinking of movements, even golf can more or less be reduced to reflex level.

[If you have been playing golf long enough it is possible to hit the ball with your eyes shut, assuming that you have taken up your stance first with eyes open.

This is muscular memory. A simple test is to close your eyes and then touch your nose with one finger. You will succeed every time. Another test is to close your eyes and try to touch the tips of the first fingers of each hand together in front of you. Most people miss for a few times until they have practised enough—the difficulty arising because both fingers are moving.

After practice muscular memory comes into play and you can do the test quite simply.]

Q. If a player does not possess the correct inherent qualities what can he do to improve matters?

A. Constant practice may help but the truth is we are more or less limited to the factors which are in-born at birth. It is possible to attain a very high standard, but in this instance we are talking about the player wishing to become either great or outstanding.

Q. Mr Henry Longhurst, the golf writer and TV commentator, has suffered from putting "yips", and over dinner made a point which is worth mentioning.

He said that a rabbit can run much faster than a stoat, yet it freezes when a stoat is near. Rather like the golfer freezes on a short putt.

I feel this is a good comparison but now I doubt whether a player can cure himself unless over a period of time his mental approach changes. How can a victim be helped to defeat the "yips"?

A. This is difficult and can only really be overcome by feeding your confidence. The best practical plan is to change your grip or your putter. For example, try a reverse grip. Making some definite physical change or grip or putter will give a different feel.

Q. Many golfers suffer from "first tee" nerves on competition day, and it doesn't help to have other players standing around watching. What should he have in mind to reduce the "butterflies" before he strikes his opening drive?

A. He must definitely repress the things around him. This can be done by thinking of one thing, be it some gimmick for the day in his swing, or just concentrating on striking the ball and putting his trust in his accepted swing.

Naturally some players are more prone to outside interference than others. What helps, as in the rest of life, is experience. Playing in more and more competitions will minimise opening-shot fears—and this applies to golfers at all levels.

Mention of a "gimmick for the day" reminded me that Henry Cotton many years ago advised club golfers to follow his own example of concentrating on one gimmick for the day.

The idea being that the player thinks about just one aspect of his swing

K*

on the round. What Henry didn't do was to outline the reason for his excellent advice.

Thinking positively of one little thing—it could be keeping the left foot on the ground a little longer or making sure the head stays still—naturally represses any outside distractions you may have around you.

In many instances the gimmick you have settled on—or had given you—will not make you hit the ball any better physically.

What it will do is remove the picture of disaster.

Let me cite an example of how anxiety or fear manifests itself. If you were asked to walk along a nine-inch wide plank resting on the ground you would do it with ease.

Put that plank 20 feet in the air and you would experience much more trouble, due to fear of falling off. Even if you were to accomplish it the chances are that your movements would be noticeably unsteady.

What has happened is that the mental picture of disaster has dominated the mental picture of success. Confidence has gone. Raise the plank in stages, say foot by foot, and your confidence would be greatly increased by the time the 20-foot level was reached.

The same thing can happen in golf.

If your game has gone sour and confidence is low, or something is amiss with your swing, make a fresh start with your short shots and work up to the big ones.

Go back to the basics and learn to walk again.

How often have you seen a player hit a bad shot and throw or break a club in anger?

I never blame such a man myself. What he is really doing is giving vent to inner feelings and breaking the tension that has built up.

My experience is that these "explosive" individuals after going into their club-bending acts very quickly calm down and play the remainder of the round quite well.

If the same individual tried to "bottle it up" his game would disintegrate from the moment of tension.

Another glaring example of repressing anxiety after playing a bad shot is provided by one of Britain's best tournament players, Dai Rees.

All the years he has been playing he has never admitted he has played a poor shot through his own deficiencies. Yet I've seen him play every bad shot in the book, including shanking.

To his way of thinking it was never his fault. It was the course to blame, the type of lie, spectators moving about or talking, bad kicks, and so forth.

I'm sure that if conditions were perfect and he hit a "rabbit" shot he would try to convince the onlookers that an aircraft was starting up 100 miles away and the noise had put him off.

Once again this is individual make-up and he sheds his anxiety by blaming everything else but himself. Feeding his confidence and not his anxiety.

This could be the reason he has been such a successful competitor. I envy him his outlook because I am one of nature's "bottle-it-up" brigade and tend to blame myself even when outside factors are largely at fault.

Just like an actor on his first night the golfer, amateur or professional, is no good unless he has some anxiety. If he lacks anxiety it means that he doesn't really care.

Anxiety expresses itself in many ways and I have known players take superstition to an extraordinary level.

One man will say he has to be immaculately dressed or he won't play clean golf. Another will clean his shoes when they don't need cleaning.

I think we're nearly all superstitious about the number of the ball we play. I don't think I could hit a No 5. I always make sure my ball is a 1, 2, 7 or 8.

I'm not sure why I don't like 3, 4, 5 or 6. Perhaps I'm thinking I don't want a five or six on my score card, whereas a one or two would be most acceptable.

A seven or eight? Well, that's tempting fate.

Caddies can have their effect also. If the caddie looks a dominating character ready to mutter silently that his Aunt Agatha could do better with a walking stick, you grow increasingly self-conscious and start wondering what that last sniff meant.

All these are mental factors—and there are many more. A consoling thought, though, is that if we were all sane in the first place would we start playing golf?

CHAPTER TWENTY

The Course Art of Golf

When all the theorising and practice has been done—and let me emphasise that I cannot play the shots for you, it's up to you to study the advice
and apply it—the game of golf boils down to how you play on the course.

What I do ask you to remember is that golf is not so much a question of
how well you can play but *how well you can play when you are playing badly*!

Nobody in the whole game can arrive on the first tee confident he is
about to hit every green in regulation figures. What is important is to be
able to return a reasonable score when you are below form.

Most people once they realise they are slightly off-song try to make up
for their errors by attempting ambitious shots well above their normal
capabilities. This only makes things worse.

Say you have topped your tee shot. The usual response is to thrash at the
second shot hoping to atone and reach the green. More often than not that
shot is topped, too.

You can play and pray for a miracle after a mistake so long as you
understand that most of the time it isn't going to happen.

In explanation of my comment about "playing well when you're playing
badly" consider the fact that we all play to a certain standard on average.
Sometimes we are a little better, more often a little worse.

But your handicap is based on your very best golf. Take the man off
13 handicap who shoots a 75 and returns a score of 62 nett. His future
handicap will be assessed on that.

Next day he may go round in 95, and a day later in 85. Now what is his
real handicap? He is likely to card more scores of 90 than 75.

He is only likely to hit his target of 75 once or twice a year, and all the
rest of the time, in relation to that good score, he is playing "badly".

So it becomes a question of how well you can play above that score. Or,
put another way, how well you can play badly.

It is always a good thing to warm up before a competition and get your-self loose prior to the opening tee shot.

The best way is to start with the irons and then go on to the woods. After which move on to the practice putting green and steady yourself down. It's the golf equivalent of the cricketer "getting his eye in".

Don't overdo the practice, though. You don't want to tire yourself out, and I think 25 shots before a big match is quite enough.

If it's a stroke-play competition then I suggest you tackle the round aggressively but bearing in mind commonsense safety limitations.

You will never have a brilliant round while adopting a policy of playing defensively. Play confident shots off the tee and once within range attack the greens with even less reservation (PLATE 54).

PLATE 54 England Cricket Skipper Colin Cowdrey had a foot injury when he posed for this "Cover Drive". He had to stand *still* and swing —being unable to put much weight on his left foot—and his swing path shows the value of doing just that.

Whatever happened on the previous hole or the last stroke—forget it. Whether you got a birdie or took seven shots is of no importance. The game of golf is entirely the next shot to be played. Don't crow or worry, just concentrate on the shot in hand.

Lots of players think their card has been ruined once they have taken an eight and mentally "tear up". But one bad hole isn't the end of it.

Admittedly the account which follows is somewhat extreme but it illus-trates the point that you should always keep trying: a man I know played in a large society meeting and started with an eagle two at the first hole.

The second hole was a par four and he took a disastrous 14. Ninety-nine out of a hundred players would have scattered the score card to the wind.

He went on to birdie the next eight holes, so that after ten holes he was all-square to par. He parred the remaining holes and won not only the handicap cup but the scratch trophy also. And that with a 14 on his card.

I know from experience that a lot of amateurs once they realise they are having a good round begin to play defensively. What they are trying to do is save what they have already collected.

That's when they start to steer the ball and get into trouble. What I advise when you are going well is to attack even harder.

When it comes to match play, the thing to remember is to play against the card and *not* against your opponent.

Why? If you play against your opponent it means you are either trying to match him shot for shot, or if he is playing badly you may start playing loosely yourself.

In a lifetime of golf if you forget the man and play against the card you will win more games than you lose. There will be exceptions to the rule, of course, say when your opponent has gone astray and it is obviously prudent to play safe. Still, if you're playing against the card you won't be playing fancy shots anyway.

Should you arrive at the happy position of being four holes up don't think the game is all over. What you should be thinking about is going five up.

It is important to get your par threes at the short holes. The common mistake is to under club and play short.

Always tee up when it is possible—it increases confidence—and whether using an iron or a wood off the tee have the ball teed only just off the ground.

If the pin is tucked behind a bunker or at one side of the green always play for the meat of the green. This policy invariably pays off.

Now for some awkward lies and situations sure to come your way in golf:

SIDE SLOPE (feet above ball). The ground is sloping away from you and from this position the customary result is a fade or push, caused by taking the club outside on the backswing and hitting across the ball, or by trying to turn into it.

The way to play the shot is to make sure the clubhead follows the line of the ground. For this, and the three shots following that I'm listing, a restricted swing is advisable.

Play a normal shot and don't try to do something consciously. Letting the clubhead follow the ground minimises any slice and aiming a little left of the pin will help to deliver the ball on target.

One final tip, a slightly sitting position at address will help.

SIDE SLOPE (ball above feet). Go down the grip a little and once again let the clubhead follow the ground.

This time a hook is likely. Adopt a more upright position and stand slightly closer to the ball than for a normal shot. Aim slightly to the right to neutralise the draw you can expect.

DOWNHILL LIE. Should you use a 7-iron then a downhill lie will automatically give it the loft of a 6-iron. The ball should be played from the middle of the feet or a little right of centre.

Keep the club low to the ground on the backswing (to avoid picking the club up too soon) and make sure you hit down and through.

At address your weight will be rather more on the left foot than the right. If it looks to be a normal 6-iron shot then use a 7-iron. The customary result of a shot from this lie is more of a low-flying ball.

And the biggest mistake is topping, caused by coming off the ball too soon.

UPHILL LIE. This is an easier shot. As you take up your stance your left leg will be bent and the right straight. There is a tendency to lean forward, and this puts the weight on your right leg.

The ball is played from just a little left of centre and the shot is likely to be high-flying. So that if a 9-iron seems enough to reach the green I would go for a 7-iron instead. Go up one or two clubs according to what experience teaches you.

Watch out for any suggestion of falling back at impact.

BEHIND A TREE. If you are really tight behind a tree then settle for a chip out sideways which will leave you in a position to attack the pin with your next shot.

If in any doubt always play within your own capabilities and go for the shot which is sure to leave your next stroke free from trouble. Don't get too ambitious.

Should the ball be far enough back from the tree for one of your clubs to carry it over the top then by all means go for this stroke.

Sometimes it seems possible to reach the green by bending the ball round the obstacle. I think you would profit by leaving this shot to the experts. Your prospect of landing in more trouble is too strong.

Much better to have a five than an eight on your card. Unfortunately, repeat unfortunately, this "bending" shot does occasionally come off for the club golfer, but far better to play the percentage shot.

UNDER A BUSH. Take a club with little loft, say a 4 or 5-iron, and since your backswing will be limited settle for a short stab shot. Go down the shaft, take a very firm grip, and have the hands a little ahead of the ball.

NEXT TO A WALL. If the situation stops you standing to the ball then try to play a left-handed shot. This is done by reversing the grip and turning the club over so that you are striking with the toe of the club.

In the appropriate situation you may prefer to play the ball at the wall at an angle so that it ricochets in the desired direction—much as a billiard ball comes off the cush.

FACING A NARROW AND TROUBLE-LINED FAIRWAY. Hitting a straight ball is the hardest shot in golf—and seems to become still harder when it is essential to play a straight ball off the tee.

What I do is to go down the grip on my driver. If you feel danger threatening I recommend that you settle for loss of distance and go down to a 3-wood or a long iron.

It is always better to play the percentage shot. By making sure you leave the ball in play the prospect is of a certain five and it is always possible you may turn it into a four.

Whatever you do avoid trying to steer the ball. Much better to stand still, keep your eye on the back of the ball, and trust your swing.

Should you be a player living with a hook or a slice then when the fairway is narrow you must sacrifice distance for accuracy.

OUT OF A DITCH. If the ditch is running in the same direction as you are hitting then it can be worth while, depending on depth of ditch and other circumstances, to attempt a shot out.

Take the longest lofted club you have got. You need a long club because you will be standing outside the ditch and bending over considerably. I usually settle for a 6-iron in such circumstances.

You should take an upright swing and the danger is of catching the sides of the ditch as you come down.

So much for tricky situations; now I think you should know some of the ploys of gamesmanship that may be tried on you.

An obvious one, already referred to, is when your opponent remarks casually on the tee how close the out-of-bounds border is. Implanting the thought is enough to make some players drive straight out of play.

Watch out for the opponent who is waiting for you to play first and while standing there makes it clear he is going to use a wood himself. He knows it's really an iron shot and once you have taken your wood he changes his club for an iron. Or, on the other hand, he stands waiting with an iron when he knows a wood is required.

Then there's the man who hits a poor putt and the ball stops halfway to the flag. "My goodness, this green's slow" he protests aloud. You fall for it and play a hard putt and go flying past.

One that I've used occasionally is asking my opponent "Do you breathe in or out when you hit the ball?" It works, and he's never the same player for the rest of that round.

You'll meet the man who has hooked his ball—and knows it. He steps off the tee and says "What a strong cross-wind. Did you see the way it took my ball?" The idea is that you will aim off target expecting the wind to do the rest.

Another seemingly innocent question is "Have you always swung like that?" It leaves you wondering what's wrong with your swing.

Or someone may say when you're going well "You're playing today better than you can." It suggests you will "blow up" shortly and starts you wondering what is your normal standard.

Another remark, mostly from the low-handicap player to a high-handicap man, is "Do you always hit the ball that far?" He wants you to start straining to impress him by hitting the ball even farther. The moment you swallow the bait you're finished.

Now what about the best way to get out of the rough? The first thing you must accept is that you probably have lost a shot. Try to achieve the impossible and you may lose still more.

You might get away with a 3-iron or 4-wood from rough but I place the odds at around 30-to-1 against.

My advice is never use from the rough the same club you would use from the fairway for the comparable distance.

One common factor with all shots from the rough is that the clubhead generally turns over at impact. The shot is smothered and invariably flies left.

There is practically no backspin and the ball will run more than it would from a fairway shot. So if the fairway shot is a 5-iron then take a 7-iron from semi-rough.

If in tough rough all you can do is use a wedge or sand iron. I always go for the heaviest club in the bag. Force the ball out rather than attempt a delicately judged shot.

Special care is needed if the ball is in heather. It may look to be sitting up nicely but the "branch stems" often turn the clubhead right round and stop it dead.

In heather I would never go beneath a 5-iron even if a 3-wood is necessary.

With all shots from the rough, and particularly when in long rough, swing the club back steeper than usual. If you take it back low the grass will wrap around the clubhead and shaft. Furthermore, a steeply descending blow gets the ball into the air sooner.

The left-hand grip must be firmer than for ordinary shots and, as more force is being used, there is a tendency for the body to come up at impact. So make sure you stay down throughout the entire swing.

The method is to position the ball more to the left side of middle and adopt a slightly open stance. This aids swinging through the ball and produces a more upright swing.

If you do succumb to temptation and use a wood or 3-iron from the rough then be sure to hold on with your left hand so that the club face stays square at impact.

When in trouble a lot of golfers play the shot quickly in order to get it out of the way. Far better to take your time and study the shot from all angles. If possible find a similar spot nearby and try a practice swing or two before moving over to the ball.

To our lady golfers I say try not to be so self-conscious and don't be shy of seeking instruction from your professional.

I think it is fear more than anything else which affects your standard of play. This is especially true when you are playing out of bunkers.

Yet you should play this shot superbly because women golfers tend to swing quite slowly. What I have noticed is that too many ladies give the impression that the club is swinging them.

If, like many other women, you are finding trouble getting the ball into the air then the most obvious reason is lack of clubhead speed.

Finally, I want to offer some thoughts on playing during winter months and in wind. A lot of golfers like to keep going through all weather and the big advantage is that it does keep the swing oiled until the new season looms.

But the combination of water-proof clothing, soft ground, little roll, and cold atmosphere means that the ball will not travel as far as it did during the summer.

Some golfers overlook that fact and grow disappointed. Just remember that the difference in distance between summer and winter is tremendous.

It could be as much as 100 yards—and no doubt accounts for so many players coming to me for lessons during the winter for the sole reason that they have lost length.

Don't slog in a search for extra distance. This only results in heaving at the ball with heavy body muscles.

If you have been suffering from some type of bad shot during the competition months then winter is a good time to ask your professional to put things right.

You'll have enough time to practise the correct movements and make them habit-forming before the next season opens.

Too many players dash in for a quick lesson in March and expect a lightning cure. This means the professional has to undo the tangle that the player has got himself into during the previous four or five months. It cannot be done that quickly.

When the grass is wet it is essential to hit the ball first. Should you hit the ground first then water or wet grass will come between clubface and ball.

The result? No grip between clubface and ball at impact, and hardly any control over the shot. One good thing about winter—you can play more target golf, and when it comes to driving you can hit the ball more off line without running into trouble than is possible during the warmer months.

When conditions are windy then widen your stance at address. This helps to maintain balance.

Position the ball a little more back towards the right foot than you would during normal play.

The purpose is to keep the ball down. Keep the clubhead low on the backswing as long as practicable and keep it low to ground after the ball has been struck.

When playing downwind still maintain your wider stance. The fault to avoid is of "leaning back" into the wind, which brings about topping. Keep your head still and, once more, low to ground on the backswing and again on the follow-through.

On a downwind shot a 6-iron, for instance, because it gets the ball into the air, will turn into a 4-iron.

Crosswind shots present more difficulty, in particular the crosswind blowing at your back as you address the ball.

If the crosswind is at your face then aim more to the right than customary and feel you are playing a straight shot. The wind will do the rest.

With the crosswind at your back then aim to the left and once again play your normal straight shot.

Don't fight the wind. One swing is enough for any man to look after. If you change your swing to meet prevailing conditions you will never be consistent and will only spoil your free swing.

CHAPTER TWENTY-ONE

A Reminder

My hope in writing this book is that it will help all classes of golfers along the path to master golf. If it does so then I will be proud to have given something back to a game which has always been so generous to me.

I am always delighted to see a keen club golfer, no matter what his handicap, playing to the best of his ability and finding enjoyment in what King James's troops used to call " 'ockey at the 'alt".

There are times when things go wrong or a big match is due when a quick reminder of the key points is useful. So to finish I offer this "top ten" guide to some of the basics that will help to get results:

1. Check your equipment. Make sure the grips are not slippery.
2. Check your grip. Have the two inverted "V's" correctly aligned.
3. Check your stance. And that also includes the position of the ball between the feet and how far you are standing from the ball.
4. Feel relaxed.
5. Concentrate on swinging rhythmically along the correct clubhead path.
6. Keep your head still. Don't sway.
7. Have a mental picture of how and where you want the ball to go.
8. Don't hit at—hit through.
9. Hold your follow-through for a few seconds after each shot.
10. Above all, trust your swing.

Here's wishing you happy golf and I hope we may meet on the course one day.

CHAPTER TWENTY-TWO

Strip Golf

Thanks to the London *Evening News* and that excellent artist George Stokes I am able to conclude with a series of illustrated strips explaining visually my teaching.

These strips appeared week-by-week in the *Evening News* in that newspaper's golf column and attracted a remarkable amount of interest and comment.

I particularly wanted to include them here and am grateful for the opportunity to do so. Should you have any remaining doubts or questions I am confident these drawings will provide the answers.

KEN ADWICK, PRO. AT SHOOTERS HILL GOLF CLUB, KENT. A TEACHER OF NATIONAL REPUTATION, KNOWN FOR HIS THOUGHTFUL ANALYSIS OF THE SWING ...

"I HAVE ALWAYS TAKEN THE VIEW THAT THE MOVEMENTS OF THE GOLF SWING ARE A RESPONSE TO SWINGING THE CLUB-HEAD WITH THE HANDS ... THE **RESULT** OF WHAT THE CLUB-HEAD IS DOING, **NOT THE CAUSE**. I CONCENTRATE ATTENTION ON CONTROL AND DIRECTION OF THE **CLUB-HEAD** ... **NOT** ON THE BODY MOVEMENTS IT BRINGS ABOUT ..."

A PLAYER THUS DEVELOPS A SENSE OF THE **PATH** THAT THE CLUB-HEAD IS TAKING THROUGHOUT THE SWING ...

I BELIEVE THAT GOOD PLAYERS RELY HEAVILY ON THE **AWARENESS** OF THIS 'GROOVE' OR PATH IN SHOTMAKING

POOR PLAYERS, HOWEVER, HAVE LITTLE SENSE OF THE 'ROUTE' OF THE CLUB HEAD, BECAUSE THEIR ATTENTION IS ELSEWHERE IN THE SWING ...

I HAVE ALWAYS BEEN INTERESTED IN THE IDEA OF 'MAPPING' THE **PATH** OF THE CLUB HEAD IN A **VISUAL** FORM, AS AN AID TO THOSE PLAYERS WHO LACK FEEL OF THE CLUB-HEAD PATH. WITH THE HELP OF A COLLEAGUE I HAVE FINALLY DONE THIS, AND THE RESULTS HAVE BEEN QUITE ASTONISHING! **A NEW AND PRECISE METHOD OF SWING ANALYSIS** HAS EMERGED.

KEN ADWICK, PRO. AT SHOOTERS HILL GOLF CLUB · KENT ...

"SINCE VISUAL IMAGES ARE A POWERFUL AID TO ALL TEACHING, I HAVE BEEN INTERESTED IN DEVISING A **VISUAL METHOD** OF RECORDING THE **PATH OF THE CLUB-HEAD** IN THE SWING, AS A MEANS OF DEVELOPING AND REINFORCING THE 'FEEL' OF SWINGING THE CLUB-HEAD ON THE DESIRED ROUTE ..."

THE METHOD, WHICH I HAVE PATENTED, EMPLOYS A LIGHT ON THE RIGHT THUMB ...

... AND ON THE CLUB-HEAD

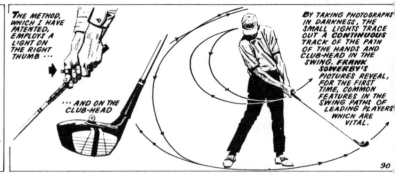

BY TAKING PHOTOGRAPHS IN DARKNESS, THE SMALL LIGHTS TRACE OUT A **CONTINUOUS** TRACK OF THE PATH OF THE HANDS AND CLUB-HEAD IN THE SWING. **FRANK SOWERBY'S** PICTURES REVEAL, FOR THE FIRST TIME, COMMON FEATURES IN THE SWING PATHS OF LEADING PLAYERS WHICH ARE VITAL.

"CONTRARY TO ACCEPTED THEORY, MY NEW 'X-RAY' SWING PICTURES HAVE REVEALED BEYOND DOUBT THAT THE DOWNSWING IS IN FACT **OUTSIDE** THE BACKSWING. TOP CLASS PLAYERS IN FACT HIT THE BALL ON A SLIGHTLY **OUT-TO-IN** PATH!

NEIL COLES, ONE OF MY 'SUBJECTS', CONFIRMED THAT WHEN HE IS PLAYING WELL, HIS DIVOTS POINT **LEFT** OF THE TARGET."

DIVOT LEFT ✓   DIVOT RIGHT ✗

WHEN HE IS PLAYING BADLY, NEIL'S DIVOTS TEND TO GO TO THE **RIGHT!**

I HAVE TAKEN SEVERAL SETS OF PICTURES OF THE SWINGS OF GOOD PLAYERS. THE OVERALL 'SHAPE' IS THE SAME, AND LOOKS LIKE THIS ...

MAIN FEATURES ARE ...

● A VERY WIDE TAKEAWAY WITH NO WRIST BREAK, OR ROLLING OF THE WRISTS

● THE BACKSWING IS CONSIDERABLY WIDER THAN THE DOWNSWING

● THE FOLLOW THROUGH IS INVARIABLY WIDE AND EXTENDED, AND LOW TO THE GROUND FOR AT LEAST A FOOT PAST IMPACT POINT

THE SWINGS OF MOST HANDICAP PLAYERS, I HAVE FOUND, LACK THESE FEATURES.

THE 'X-RAY' SWINGS OF TOP PLAYERS AND HANDICAPPERS DIFFER WIDELY, REVEALING SPECIFIC FEATURES THAT ARE ABSENT FROM THE SWINGS OF AVERAGE PLAYERS. I INTEND TO SHOW HOW THESE DESIRABLE 'PRO' FEATURES CAN BE ACQUIRED

THE AVERAGE HANDICAPPER'S SWING 'SHAPE' LOOKS LIKE THIS ...

WHEN COMPARED WITH THE 'PRO' SWING SHAPE, WE NOTE THE FOLLOWING ...

HANDICAPPER'S SWING

● THE TAKEAWAY IS NARROW, AS OPPOSED TO WIDE, INDICATING EARLY WRIST-COCK, AND POSSIBLY ALSO WRIST-ROLL

● THE DOWNSWING IS CONSEQUENTLY ONLY SLIGHTLY NARROWER THAN THE BACKSWING, HENCE, LOSS OF DISTANCE

● THE DOWNSWING IS MUCH **STEEPER**, INDICATING STIFF WRISTS AND A RELUCTANCE TO RELEASE THE CLUB-HEAD

● THE FOLLOW THROUGH IS LESS EXTENDED, AND RISES UP MORE STEEPLY, OFF THE LINE OF FLIGHT

Panel 1 (top left)

"MY ADVICE TO HANDICAPPERS, BASED ON THE EVIDENCE OF MY 'X-RAY' SWING PICTURES, IS TO **CONTINUE** TO HAVE THE **FEELING** THAT YOU ARE STRIKING THE BALL FROM THE 'INSIDE', ALTHOUGH WE KNOW THAT GOOD PLAYERS HIT SLIGHTLY OUT-TO-IN. I ADVISE THIS BECAUSE THE HANDICAPPER'S FAULT IS THAT HE HITS **TOO MUCH** OUTSIDE ...

...WITH CONSEQUENT PULL OR SLICE ..."

INSIDE

OUTSIDE

Panel 2 (top middle)

SECOND, CONCENTRATE ON ELIMINATING WRIST-ROLL AND WRIST-COCK ON THE TAKEAWAY. THIS WILL SET UP THE **WIDE** BACKSWING ARC THAT WE ARE LOOKING FOR TO INCREASE DISTANCE ...

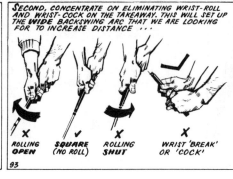

ROLLING **OPEN** X · **SQUARE** (NO ROLL) ✓ · ROLLING **SHUT** X · WRIST 'BREAK' OR 'COCK' X

93

Panel 3 (top right)

DO NOT, HOWEVER, 'REACH' BACK WITH THE CLUB-HEAD AND THE LEFT SIDE AND CAUSE A **SWAY** AWAY FROM THE BALL ...

Panel 4 (row 2 left)

"MY 'X-RAY' SWING PICTURES INDICATE CLEARLY, AS I HAVE ALWAYS MAINTAINED, THAT THE WRISTS DO NOT BREAK— OR 'COCK' — FULLY UNTIL THE BACKSWING HAS BEEN **COMPLETED**, AND THE CLUB IS ON ITS WAY BACK TO THE BALL ..."

94

IN OTHER WORDS, IT IS THE **INERTIA**, OR 'DRAG' OF THE CLUB-HEAD IN THE PAUSE BETWEEN BACKSWING AND DOWNSWING THAT CAUSES THE WRISTS TO 'COCK'

CHANGE OF DIRECTION OF CLUB-HEAD CAUSES WRISTS TO COCK

Panel 5 (row 2 right)

THIS IS AN ENTIRELY NATURAL EVENT, AND REQUIRES NO CONSCIOUS EFFORT. DO NOT INTERRUPT THIS SPONTANEOUS INCIDENT BY COCKING THE WRISTS ON THE BACKSWING. LET THE WRISTS REMAIN **PASSIVE** ON THE TAKE-AWAY AND BACKSWING ...

EARLY WRIST-COCK ON BACKSWING. **WRONG**

NO CONSCIOUS WRIST-COCK. **RIGHT**

Panel 6 (row 3 left)

"**THE** FACT THAT THE DOWNSWING OF A GOOD PLAYER IS CONSIDERABLY **NARROWER** THAN THE BACKSWING MAY INDUCE THE HANDICAPPER TO ATTEMPT TO 'HIT-LATE', OR **DELAY** THE 'UNCOCKING' OF THE WRISTS. **DON'T DO IT!**

95

ANY ATTEMPT TO 'HIT-LATE' IS AN INVITATION TO DISASTER. IT WILL LEAVE THE CLUB-FACE **WIDE OPEN** ON IMPACT ...

FACE OPEN

Panel 7 (row 3 middle)

YOUR PROBLEM IS TO HIT **EARLY ENOUGH**, TO GET THE CLUB-HEAD IN SQUARE TO THE BALL **IN TIME!**

Panel 8 (row 3 right)

FROM THE TOP OF THE BACKSWING, THINK ABOUT GETTING THE CLUB-HEAD BACK TO THE BALL **IN PHASE** WITH YOUR HANDS. **DISCOURAGE** THE FEELING OF THE CLUB-HEAD **TRAILING** THE HANDS. RATHER, GET THE CLUB-HEAD BACK TO THE BALL **FIRST!**

GET CLUB-HEAD IN FIRST (EARLY)

Panel 9 (row 4 left)

"MY 'X-RAY' SWING PICTURES HAVE REVEALED THAT THE HANDICAP GOLFER'S DOWNSWING IS **MUCH STEEPER** THAN THAT OF THE GOOD PLAYER. THIS INDICATES A FAILURE TO 'STAY BEHIND THE BALL' UNTIL IMPACT OCCURS, PRODUCING A CHOPPING ACTION, AND A POOR CONTACT WITH THE BALL ..."

I HAVE ALWAYS MAINTAINED THAT THE WEIGHT IS **NOT** TRANSFERRED TO THE LEFT FOOT UNTIL **AFTER THE BALL HAS BEEN STRUCK**. MY PICTURES PROVE IT ...

Panel 10 (row 4 right)

THE WEIGHT MOVES OVER **AFTER** IMPACT. ANY ATTEMPT TO SHIFT THE WEIGHT DURING OR BEFORE IMPACT DISSIPATES POWER **AND** PLACES THE BODY AND HANDS **AHEAD** OF CLUB-HEAD AND BALL ... CAUSING **SLICE** ...

WEIGHT SHIFT BEFORE IMPACT

OPEN CLUB-FACE

96

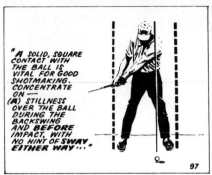

"*A* SOLID, SQUARE CONTACT WITH THE BALL IS VITAL FOR GOOD SHOTMAKING. CONCENTRATE ON —
(A) STILLNESS OVER THE BALL DURING THE BACKSWING AND BEFORE IMPACT, WITH NO HINT OF SWAY EITHER WAY ..."

97

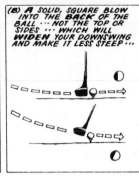

(B) A SOLID, SQUARE BLOW INTO THE BACK OF THE BALL ... NOT THE TOP OR SIDES ... WHICH WILL WIDEN YOUR DOWNSWING AND MAKE IT LESS STEEP ...

(C) A SLOW, CONTROLLED SWING, TO GIVE YOURSELF TIME AND A STEADY BASE TO HIT THE BALL SOLIDLY, OFF THE CENTRE OF THE CLUB-FACE.

ACCURATE AND SOLID STRIKING WILL PRODUCE MORE DISTANCE THAN POWER OR SPEED OF SWING!

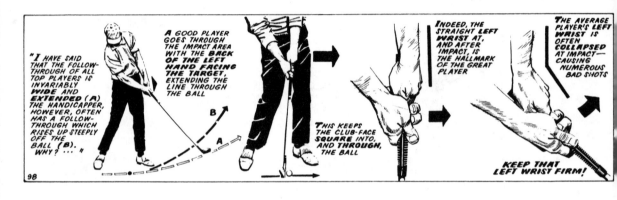

"*I* HAVE SAID THAT THE FOLLOW-THROUGH OF ALL TOP PLAYERS IS INVARIABLY WIDE AND EXTENDED (A) THE HANDICAPPER, HOWEVER, OFTEN HAS A FOLLOW-THROUGH WHICH RISES UP STEEPLY OFF THE BALL (B). WHY? ..."

98

A GOOD PLAYER GOES THROUGH THE IMPACT AREA WITH THE BACK OF THE LEFT HAND FACING THE TARGET, EXTENDING THE LINE THROUGH THE BALL

THIS KEEPS THE CLUB-FACE SQUARE INTO, AND THROUGH, THE BALL

INDEED, THE STRAIGHT LEFT WRIST AT, AND AFTER IMPACT, IS THE HALLMARK OF THE GREAT PLAYER

THE AVERAGE PLAYER'S LEFT WRIST IS OFTEN COLLAPSED AT IMPACT — CAUSING NUMEROUS BAD SHOTS

KEEP THAT LEFT WRIST FIRM!

"*I* HAVE ALWAYS STRESSED THE ROLE OF THE HANDS IN THE GOLF SWING. A FIRM LEFT ARM AND WRIST AT IMPACT ... AND BEYOND ... PRODUCES A SUSTAINED BLOW THROUGH THE BALL ... ON TO THE TARGET ... MAKING FOR DISTANCE AND ACCURACY ..."

99

LONG AFTER THE BALL HAS BEEN STRUCK, THE LEFT ARM AND WRIST REMAINS FIRM KEEPING THE CLUB-HEAD ON LINE

HERE, THE LEFT WRIST HAS COLLAPSED, A SURE SIGN OF A FAULTY HAND ACTION AT IMPACT ... OFTEN CAUSED BY THE MISTAKEN IDEA THAT THE WRISTS ARE 'ROLLED' THROUGH THE IMPACT ZONE

IN A GOOD SWING THE LEFT ARM AND WRIST REMAIN FIRM LONG AFTER THE BALL HAS GONE. THE WRISTS DO NOT ROLL, ONLY THE FORE-ARMS CROSS IN A 'SCISSORS' ACTION

"*THE* IMPORTANCE OF A CORRECT FINISH IS OFTEN NEGLECTED BY CLUB GOLFERS. THEY CANNOT SEE HOW A MOVEMENT THAT OCCURS AFTER IMPACT CAN INFLUENCE THE SHOT. THIS IS A MISTAKE! A GOOD FINISH IS THE PRODUCT OF A SOUND SWING."

100

I HAVE ADVISED A STRAIGHT HIT THROUGH THE BALL, WITH THE BACK OF THE LEFT HAND FACING THE TARGET ...

THE LEFT WRIST REMAINS FIRM - TAKING THE CLUB HEAD OUT IN A WIDE ARC AFTER THE BALL. THIS AIDS ACCURACY AND DISTANCE, AND CREATES THE CONDITIONS WHICH WE RECOGNISE AS A 'CORRECT FINISH' POSITION ...

THESE ARE ... WEIGHT ON THE LEFT FOOT, WITH THE HANDS HIGH POSITIONED ABOVE THE LEFT EAR. REMEMBER, A CORRECT FINISH INDICATES THAT THE CLUB-HEAD HAS TRAVELLED ON THE CORRECT PATH THROUGH IMPACT!

Panel 101

"I HAVE ALWAYS STRESSED THE ROLE OF THE **HANDS** IN THE GOLF SWING. THE **HANDS SWING THE CLUB** AND THE BODY MOVEMENTS ARE MERELY A RESPONSE TO WHAT THE HANDS **ARE DOING**. I KNOW OF NO, SURER, FASTER WAY OF IMPROVING A PLAYER'S GAME THAN THE FOLLOWING EXERCISE ..."

TAKE UP YOUR STANCE WITH THE **FEET TOGETHER** (ANKLES TOUCHING), AND HIT BALLS WITH A MID IRON ...

THE BODY IS NEUTRALISED, AND THE **HANDS** ASSUME THEIR CORRECT ROLE

ONCE LET THE BODY TAKE CONTROL OF THE SWING AND YOU WILL **LOSE BALANCE!**

LET THE HANDS DO THE WORK!

SPEND ONLY A FEW SESSIONS ON THIS EXERCISE AND THE RESULTS WILL AMAZE YOU. **ACCURACY** WILL IMPROVE **WITHOUT LOSS OF DISTANCE!** THEN, WHEN YOU TAKE YOUR NORMAL STANCE YOUR **HANDS** WILL PERFORM CORRECTLY, AND THE BODY WILL **ASSUME ITS SECONDARY ROLE**

101

Panel 102

"BEFORE FAULTS ARE CORRECTED, A PLAYER MUST HAVE A **CLEAR UNDERSTANDING** OF THEIR **CAUSE**. THE **PULL** AND THE **SLICE** ARE PRODUCTS OF THE SAME BASIC SWING FAULT ... AN **OUT-TO-IN** SWING PATH.

FIRST, LET'S CLARIFY WHAT AN OUT-TO-IN PATH IS ..."

SIMPLY, IT IS A **CUT** FROM **RIGHT** TO **LEFT** (INDICATED BY THE BLACK ARROW) **ACROSS** THE INTENDED LINE OF FLIGHT OF THE BALL ...

LEFT   RIGHT

THIS SWING PATH COMBINED WITH AN **OPEN** FACE AT IMPACT CAUSES A **SLICE** ... OR A SHOT THAT CURVES WILDLY TO THE **RIGHT**

SLICE   OPEN

HOWEVER, THIS SWING PATH COMBINED WITH A FACE **SQUARE TO THE PATH OF THE SWING** (BUT CLOSED TO THE INTENDED LINE OF FLIGHT) CAUSES A **PULL** ... OR A **STRAIGHT** SHOT TO THE **LEFT** OF THE TARGET ...

PULL

SQUARE TO LINE OF FLIGHT

CLOSED TO INTENDED LINE

102

Panel 103

"I HAVE SAID THAT BOTH THE **PULL** AND **SLICE** ARE CAUSED BY AN **OUT-TO-IN** SWING PATH, SO COMMON AMONG LONG HANDICAPPERS. AN OUT-TO-IN ACTION IS SET UP BY STARTING THE DOWNSWING WITH A TURN OF THE **SHOULDERS** — AMONG OTHER THINGS. **EACH** PLAYER MUST, OF COURSE, BE ANALYSED **INDIVIDUALLY**, BUT I CAN SUGGEST A GENERAL CONCEPT TO GET THE CLUB-HEAD MOVING ON THE RIGHT PATH."

FIRST, CHECK YOUR GRIP. CHANCES ARE YOUR RIGHT HAND IS TOO MUCH ON **TOP OF THE SHAFT** (A)

A   B

... BE SURE THE "Vs" POINT TO THE **RIGHT** SHOULDER (B)

NEXT, CHECK **ALIGNMENT** TO THE **TARGET**. ARE YOUR FEET, HIPS OR SHOULDERS **OPEN?** (A) IF SO, **SQUARE UP**, FOR THIS IS **ABSOLUTELY VITAL!** (B)

A   B

NOW, KEEPING THE CLUB-HEAD **LOW** TO THE GROUND ON THE TAKEAWAY ... NO 'PICKING UP' OF THE CLUB WITH THE HANDS, REMEMBER ... HAVE THE **FEELING** OF SWINGING ON AN INCLINED PLANE **AROUND** THE BODY — AND UP **BEHIND THE HEAD** ...

103

Panel 104

"STARTING DOWN FROM THE TOP OF THE BACKSWING IS A **CRITICAL** PHASE IN THE SWING. RATHER THAN DEFINE SPECIFIC MOVEMENTS AND POSITIONS TO MASTER, I WANT TO ASK YOU TO CONSIDER THE **PATH OF THE CLUB-HEAD** TO THE IMPACT AREA, AND THROUGH THE BALL ..."

HAVE THE **FEELING** THAT YOU ARE SWINGING THE CLUB-HEAD DOWN AND **AWAY** FROM YOURSELF THROUGH IMPACT ...

... SO THAT AFTER IMPACT, THE CLUB-HEAD IS MOVING OUT TO THE **RIGHT** OF THE TARGET. IT WILL NOT DO THIS IN REALITY ... BUT THIS IS THE **FEELING** WE WANT ...

LEFT   RIGHT

THIS IS A **SURE WAY** TO PREVENT THE SHOULDERS TURNING **OPEN** ON THE DOWNSWING, WHICH CAUSES THE OUT-TO-IN PATH WE ARE SEEKING TO AVOID

BY CONCENTRATING ON THE **PATH** OF THE CLUB-HEAD THROUGH IMPACT, YOU WILL FIND THAT THE **RIGHT SHOULDER STAYS BACK** ... BEHIND THE HEAD AS IT WERE ... WHERE IT SHOULD BE!

104

"TO CURE AN OUT-TO-IN SWING, THINK OF THE UPPER BODY AS A CYLINDER. IN A TYPICAL 'SLICE SITUATION', THE UPPER BODY GETS AHEAD OF THE HANDS ... THE HEAD SLIDES TOWARDS THE TARGET AND THE RIGHT SHOULDER WHEELS ROUND WITH IT. AT IMPACT, WE SEE THE **BASE** OF THE CYLINDER, AS IT WERE ... "

THE OUT-TO-IN PATH THUS CREATED PRODUCES AN UGLY, UNCONTROLLED "SPIN"FINISH LIKE THIS—

105

RATHER, WE SHOULD SEE THE **TOP** OF THE CYLINDER AT IMPACT, WITH HEAD AND RIGHT SHOULDER HELD **BACK**— RIGHT ARM STILL **INSIDE** THE LEFT

LEADING TO A **HIGH**, WELL BALANCED, SOLID "ON LINE" FINISH LIKE THIS ...

I NEVER ASK PUPILS TO GET THEMSELVES INTO 'POSED' BODY POSITIONS. ALL THESE DESIRABLE FEATURES **HAPPEN** WHEN YOU SWING THE CLUB-HEAD ON THE RIGHT **PATH**. REMEMBER— DOWN AND **AWAY** FROM YOURSELF!

"I AM SURE THAT MANY HANDICAPPERS WILL BE SURPRISED TO LEARN THAT THE **HOOK** AND **PUSH** ARE CLOSELY RELATED. BOTH ARE THE PRODUCT OF AN '**IN-TO-OUT**' SWING PATH . THE PUSH ... A SHOT THAT FLIES **STRAIGHT**, BUT TO THE **RIGHT** OF THE TARGET... IS OFTEN WRONGLY ASSUMED TO BE A 'WEAK SLICE'. THIS INCORRECT DIAGNOSIS LEADS TO THE WRONG 'CURE'..."

106

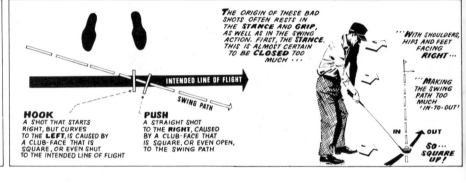

HOOK
A SHOT THAT STARTS RIGHT, BUT CURVES TO THE **LEFT**, IS CAUSED BY A CLUB-FACE THAT IS SQUARE, OR EVEN SHUT TO THE INTENDED LINE OF FLIGHT

PUSH
A STRAIGHT SHOT, CAUSED BY A CLUB-FACE THAT IS SQUARE, OR EVEN OPEN, TO THE SWING PATH

INTENDED LINE OF FLIGHT

SWING PATH

THE ORIGIN OF THESE BAD SHOTS OFTEN RESTS IN THE **STANCE** AND **GRIP**, AS WELL AS IN THE SWING ACTION. FIRST, THE **STANCE**. THIS IS ALMOST CERTAIN TO BE **CLOSED** TOO MUCH ...

... WITH SHOULDERS, HIPS AND FEET FACING **RIGHT** ...

...MAKING THE SWING PATH TOO MUCH 'IN-TO-OUT' ...

IN ─ OUT

SO ... SQUARE UP!

"A 'STRONG' GRIP ... ONE IN WHICH THREE OR FOUR KNUCKLES OF THE LEFT HAND ARE VISIBLE ... TENDS TO PROMOTE A **HOOK**. THIS GRIP BRINGS THE CLUB-FACE INTO THE IMPACT AREA IN A 'CLOSED' POSITION. HENCE THE **HOOK** ... "

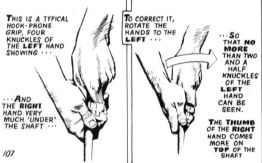

THIS IS A TYPICAL HOOK-PRONE GRIP, FOUR KNUCKLES OF THE **LEFT** HAND SHOWING ...

...AND THE **RIGHT** HAND VERY MUCH 'UNDER' THE SHAFT ...

107

TO CORRECT IT, ROTATE THE HANDS TO THE **LEFT** ...

...SO THAT **NO MORE** THAN TWO AND A HALF KNUCKLES OF THE **LEFT** HAND CAN BE SEEN. THE **THUMB** OF THE **RIGHT** HAND COMES MORE ON **TOP** OF THE SHAFT

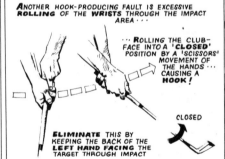

ANOTHER HOOK-PRODUCING FAULT IS EXCESSIVE **ROLLING** OF THE **WRISTS** THROUGH THE IMPACT AREA ...

...ROLLING THE CLUB-FACE INTO A 'CLOSED' POSITION BY A 'SCISSORS' MOVEMENT OF THE HANDS ... CAUSING A **HOOK**!

CLOSED

ELIMINATE THIS BY KEEPING THE BACK OF THE **LEFT HAND** FACING THE TARGET THROUGH IMPACT

" THE PLAYER WHO TENDS TO HOOK USUALLY STANDS **TOO FAR** AWAY FROM THE BALL, AND SWINGS THE CLUB **AROUND** HIS BODY IN A VERY 'FLAT' SWING PLANE ... "

HE STARTS THE TAKEAWAY ON A PRONOUNCED **INSIDE** PATH ...

...PRODUCING A VERY 'FLAT' TOP OF THE SWING POSITION, WITH THE CLUB-FACE 'SHUT' ...

THIS MAKES A **HOOK** ALMOST A CERTAINTY

RATHER, HE SHOULD STAND **CLOSER** TO THE BALL AND CONCENTRATE ON A TAKEAWAY **STRAIGHT BACK** FROM THE BALL ...

INSIDE

THIS LEADS TO A MORE UPRIGHT SWING, WITH A SQUARE FACE ...

...FROM THIS POSITION THE PLAYER SHOULD SWING DOWN ...**UNDER** HIMSELF, RATHER THAN **ROUND**— ELIMINATING HOOK.

108

"WE HAVE SAID THAT A PLAYER WHO HOOKS SHOULD DEVELOP THE FEELING THAT HE IS SWINGING THE CLUB-HEAD UP HIGH ON THE BACKSWING — AND UNDER ON THE DOWNSWING, RATHER THAN ROUND THE BODY IN A ROTARY ACTION ···"

THIS ROTARY SWING BRINGS THE CLUB-FACE INTO THE BALL VERY MUCH FROM THE INSIDE ···

IMPARTING ANTI-CLOCKWISE (HOOK) SPIN TO THE BALL ···

INSIDE

109

TO OVERCOME THIS, HE SHOULD CONCENTRATE ON SWINGING THE CLUB-HEAD DOWN ··· AND **ALONG THE LINE OF FLIGHT** ··· WITH **NO ROLLING OF THE WRISTS** ···

STRAIGHT THRO'

BY KEEPING THE BACK OF THE LEFT HAND FACING THE TARGET THRO' IMPACT, THE FACE REMAINS **SQUARE**, AND THE SWING PATH STAYS ON LINE ··· ELIMINATING HOOK

"YOUR HANDS ARE THE KEY TO THE WHOLE SWING. POWER IS CREATED BY THE BODY BUT DELIVERED TO THE BALL BY THE HANDS — VIA THE CLUB-HEAD. IF THE HANDS ARE WEAK, THEY ARE OVERPOWERED BY THE BODY, AND THEIR CONTROLLING AND GUIDING ROLE IS RENDERED IMPOSSIBLE. A CHAIN IS ONLY AS STRONG AS ITS WEAKEST LINK."

CHECK YOUR GRIP OFTEN — AND APPLY ONLY **LIGHT** PRESSURE IN THE GRIP. TENSE HANDS ARE **DEAD** HANDS ···

110

EXERCISE THE HANDS REGULARLY, BY SQUEEZING A RUBBER BALL, OR WITH SOME OTHER HAND-TRAINING DEVICE ···

··· **THEY MUST BE STRONG** TO TRANSMIT THE POWER OF THE BODY TO THE BALL

REGULARLY EMPLOY THE 'FEET TOGETHER' EXERCISE SUGGESTED EARLIER. I KNOW OF NO BETTER WAY OF SCHOOLING THE HANDS IN THEIR **CORRECT** ROLE ···

··· AND CARRY THE 'FEEL' OF THIS EXERCISE TO YOUR NORMAL SWING

"GOLF IS NOT REALLY A HOPELESSLY DIFFICULT GAME. PROGRESS LARGELY DEPENDS ON ATTENTION TO A FEW IMPORTANT BASICS — AND ELIMINATION OF UNIMPORTANT AND HARMFUL ADVICE. I WANT TO END THIS SERIES ON A SIMPLE AND POSITIVE NOTE, — IT IS —

MOST TROUBLE STARTS FROM THE TOP OF THE SWING. FROM HERE, JUST THINK OF SWINGING THE CLUB-HEAD **DOWN** INTO THE **BACK** OF THE BALL ···

··· SO THAT IT IS MOVING **STRAIGHT** TOWARDS THE **TARGET** THROUGH THE **HITTING AREA** — AND **BEYOND**. **THIS IS VITAL!**

ALLOW THE WEIGHT TO SHIFT TO THE LEFT **ONLY AFTER THE BALL HAS GONE**. THE CLUB-HEAD NOW COMES UP QUITE **NATURALLY** TO A HIGH FINISH

THE HANDS ARE CONTROLLING **DIRECTION** AND **POSITION** (OPEN, CLOSED, SQUARE) OF THE **CLUB-HEAD**. FORGET WHAT YOUR BODY IS DOING. LET IT **RESPOND FREELY** TO WHAT THE HANDS ARE DOING! **THEN YOUR GOLF IMPROVES**

111